IARIA

ICIW 2018

The Thirteenth International Conference on Internet and Web Applications and Services

July 22 - 26, 2018

Barcelona, Spain

ICIW 2018 Editors

Paulo Caetano da Silva, Salvador University (UNIFACS), Brazil
Maurício Codesso, University of Santa Catarina, Brazil

Printed from e-media with permission by:

Curran Associates, Inc.
57 Morehouse Lane
Red Hook, NY 12571

Some format issues inherent in the e-media version may also appear in this print version.

Printed by Curran Associates, Inc. (2018)

International Academy, Research, and Industry Association (IARIA)
412 Derby Way
Wilmington, DE 19810

Phone: (408) 893-6407
Fax: (408) 527-6351

petre@iaria.org

Additional copies of this publication are available from:

Curran Associates, Inc.
57 Morehouse Lane
Red Hook, NY 12571 USA
Phone: 845-758-0400
Fax: 845-758-2633
Email: curran@proceedings.com
Web: www.proceedings.com

Table of Contents

ICIW 2018

Foreword

The Thirteenth International Conference on Internet and Web Applications and Services (ICIW 2018), held between July 22 - 26, 2018- Barcelona, Spain, continued a series of co-located events that covered the complementary aspects related to designing and deploying of applications based on IP&Web techniques and mechanisms.

Internet and Web-based technologies led to new frameworks, languages, mechanisms and protocols for Web applications design and development. Interaction between web-based applications and classical applications requires special interfaces and exposes various performance parameters.

Web Services and applications are supported by a myriad of platforms, technologies, and mechanisms for syntax (mostly XML-based) and semantics (Ontology, Semantic Web). Special Web Services based applications such as e-Commerce, e-Business, P2P, multimedia, and GRID enterprise-related, allow design flexibility and easy to develop new services. The challenges consist of service discovery, announcing, monitoring and management; on the other hand, trust, security, performance and scalability are desirable metrics under exploration when designing such applications.

Entertainment systems became one of the most business-oriented and challenging area of distributed real-time software applications' and special devices' industry. Developing entertainment systems and applications for a unique user or multiple users requires special platforms and network capabilities.

Particular traffic, QoS/SLA, reliability and high availability are some of the desired features of such systems. Real-time access raises problems of user identity, customized access, and navigation. Particular services such interactive television, car/train/flight games, music and system distribution, and sport entertainment led to ubiquitous systems. These systems use mobile, wearable devices, and wireless technologies.

Interactive game applications require particular methodologies, frameworks, platforms, tools and languages. State-of-the-art games today can embody the most sophisticated technology and the most fully developed applications of programming capabilities available in the public domain.

The impact on millions of users via the proliferation of peer-to-peer (P2P) file sharing networks such as eDonkey, Kazaa and Gnutella was rapidly increasing and seriously influencing business models (online services, cost control) and user behavior (download profile). An important fraction of the Internet traffic belongs to P2P applications.

P2P applications run in the background of user's PCs and enable individual users to act as downloaders, uploaders, file servers, etc. Designing and implementing P2P applications raise particular requirements. On the one hand, there are aspects of programming, data handling, and intensive computing applications; on the other hand, there are problems of special protocol features and networking, fault tolerance, quality of service, and application adaptability.

Additionally, P2P systems require special attention from the security point of view. Trust, reputation, copyrights, and intellectual property are also relevant for P2P applications.
On-line communications frameworks and mechanisms allow distribute the workload, share business process, and handle complex partner profiles. This requires protocols supporting interactivity and real-time metrics.

Collaborative systems based on online communications support collaborative groups and are based on the theory and formalisms for group interactions. Group synergy in cooperative networks includes online gambling, gaming, and children groups, and at a larger scale, B2B and B2P cooperation.

Collaborative systems allow social networks to exist; within groups and between groups there are problems of privacy, identity, anonymity, trust, and confidentiality. Additionally, conflict, delegation, group selection, and communications costs in collaborative groups have to be monitored and managed. Building online social networks requires mechanism on popularity context, persuasion, as well as technologies, techniques, and platforms to support all these paradigms.

Also, the age of information and communication has revolutionized the way companies do business, especially in providing competitive and innovative services. Business processes not only integrates departments and subsidiaries of enterprises but also are extended across organizations and to interact with governments. On the other hand, wireless technologies and peer-to-peer networks enable ubiquitous access to services and information systems with scalability. This results in the removal of barriers of market expansion and new business opportunities as well as threats. In this new globalized and ubiquitous environment, it is of increasing importance to consider legal and social aspects in business activities and information systems that will provide some level of certainty. There is a broad spectrum of vertical domains where legal and social issues influence the design and development of information systems, such as web personalization and protection of users privacy in service provision, intellectual property rights protection when designing and implementing virtual works and multiplayer digital games, copyright protection in collaborative environments, automation of contracting and contract monitoring on the web, protection of privacy in location-based computing, etc.

We take here the opportunity to warmly thank all the members of the ICIW 2018 Technical Program Committee, as well as the numerous reviewers. The creation of such a broad and high quality conference program would not have been possible without their involvement. We also kindly thank all the authors who dedicated much of their time and efforts to contribute to ICIW 2018. We truly believe that, thanks to all these efforts, the final conference program consisted of top quality contributions.

Also, this event could not have been a reality without the support of many individuals, organizations, and sponsors. We are grateful to the members of the ICIW 2018 organizing committee for their help in handling the logistics and for their work to make this professional meeting a success.

We hope that ICIW 2018 was a successful international forum for the exchange of ideas and results between academia and industry and for the promotion of progress in the field of Internet and Web applications and services.

We are convinced that the participants found the event useful and communications very open. We hope that Barcelona provided a pleasant environment during the conference and everyone saved some time to enjoy the charm of the city.

ICIW 2018 Chairs:

ICIW Steering Committee
Stefanos Gritzalis, University of the Aegean, Greece
Sebastien Salva, UCA (Clermont Auvergne University), France
Raj Jain, Washington University in St. Louis, USA
Jian Yu, Auckland University of Technology, New Zealand
Christoph Meinel, Hasso-Plattner-Institut GmbH, Germany

ICIW Industry/Research Advisory Committee
José Luis Izkara, TECNALIA, Spain
Christos J. Bouras, University of Patras, Greece
Alex Ng, Internet Commerce Security Laboratory, Australia
Rema Hariharan, eBay, USA
Mustafa Rafique, IBM Research, Ireland

ICIW 2018

COMMITTEE

ICIW Steering Committee

Stefanos Gritzalis, University of the Aegean, Greece
Sebastien Salva, UCA (Clermont Auvergne University), France
Raj Jain, Washington University in St. Louis, USA
Jian Yu, Auckland University of Technology, New Zealand
Christoph Meinel, Hasso-Plattner-Institut GmbH, Germany

ICIW Industry/Research Advisory Committee

José Luis Izkara, TECNALIA, Spain
Christos J. Bouras, University of Patras, Greece
Alex Ng, Internet Commerce Security Laboratory, Australia
Rema Hariharan, eBay, USA
Mustafa Rafique, IBM Research, Ireland

ICIW 2018 Technical Program Committee

Mohd Helmy Abd Wahab, Universiti Tun Hussein Onn, Malaysia
Witold Abramowicz, Poznan University of Economics and Business, Poland
Mehmet Aktas, Yildiz Technical University, Turkey
Grigore Albeanu, Spiru Haret University - Bucharest, Romania
Markus Aleksy, ABB AG, Germany
Pedro Álvarez, University of Zaragoza, Spain
Leonidas Anthopoulos, University of Applied Science (TEI) of Thessaly, Greece
Filipe Araujo, University of Coimbra, Portugal
Ezzy Ariwa, University of Bedfordshire, UK
Jocelyn Aubert, Luxembourg Institute of Science and Technology (LIST), Luxembourg
Arnim Bleier, GESIS - Leibniz Institute for the Social Sciences, Germany
Masoud Barati, Sherbrooke University, Canada
Andres Baravalle, University of East London, UK
Dan Benta, Agora University of Oradea, Romania
Luis Bernardo, Universidade NOVA de Lisboa, Portugal
Christos J. Bouras, University of Patras, Greece
Mahmoud Brahimi, University of Msila, Algeria
Tharrenos Bratitsis, University of Western Macedonia, Greece
Paulo Caetano da Silva, Salvador University - UNIFACS, Brazil
Jorge C. S. Cardoso, University of Coimbra, Portugal
Dickson Chiu, The University of Hong Kong, Hong Kong
Soon Ae Chun, City University of New York, USA
Marta Cimitile, Unitelma Sapienza University, Italy
Gianpiero Costantino, Institute of Informatics and Telematics (IIT) - National Research Council (CNR), Italy

Giuseppe A. Di Lucca, University of Sannio | RCOST (Research Center on Software Technology), Italy
Ronaldo dos Santos Mello, Federal University of Santa Catarina, Brazil
Luis Espinosa-Anke, Cardiff University, UK
Javier Fabra, Universidad de Zaragoza, Spain
Muhammad Fahad, Universite Lumiere LYON 2, France
Johannes Fähndrich, Technische Universität Berlin, Germany
Stefan Fischer, University of Lübeck, Germany
Karla Donato Fook, IFMA - Maranhao Federal Institute for Education, Science and Technology, Brazil
Panayotis Fouliras, University of Macedonia, Greece
Ivan Ganchev, University of Limerick, Ireland / Plovdiv University "Paisii Hilendarski", Bulgaria
Marcos Garcia, University of Coruña, Galicia, Spain
Mohamed Gharzouli, University of Abdelhamid Mehri Constantine 2, Algeria
Nizar Ghoula, Yellow pages Group, Montreal, Canada
Katja Gilly de la Sierra - Llamazares, Universidad Miguel Hernández, Spain
Patrizia Grifoni, National Research Council, Italy
Stefanos Gritzalis, University of the Aegean, Greece
Carlos Guerrero, University of Balearic Islands, Spain
Bidyut Gupta, Southern Illinois University, USA
Ileana Hamburg, Institut Arbeit und Technik, Germany
Rema Hariharan, eBay, USA
Mamoun Abu Helou, Al Istiqlal University, Palestine
Martin Henkel, Stockholm University, Sweden
José Luis Herrero, University of Extremadura, Spain
Tzung-Pei Hong, National University of Kaohsiung, Taiwan
Arthur Huang, Tarleton State University, USA
Emilio Insfran, Universitat Politecnica de Valencia, Spain
Naghmeh Ivaki, University of Coimbra, Portugal
José Luis Izkara, TECNALIA, Spain
Raj Jain, Washington University in St. Louis, USA
Marc Jansen, University of Applied Sciences Ruhr West, Germany
Jehn-Ruey Jiang, National Central University, Taiwan
Dimitris Karagiannis, University of Vienna, Austria
Sokratis K. Katsikas, Center for Cyber & Information Security | Norwegian University of Science & Technology (NTNU), Norway
Selma Khouri, ESI, Algeria / ENSMA, France
Mark Kibanov, University of Kassel, Germany
Suhyun Kim, KIST (Korea Institute of Science and Technology), South Korea
Samad Kolahi, Unitec Institute of Technology, New Zealand
George Koutromanos, National and Kapodistrian University of Athens, Greece
Sarasi Lalithsena, Kno.e.sis Center | Wright State University, USA
José Laurindo Campos dos Santos, Instituto Nacional de Pesquisas da Amazônia, Brazil
Longzhuang Li, Texas A&M University-Corpus Christi, USA
David Lizcano Casas, Open University of Madrid (UDIMA), Spain
Malamati Louta, University of Western Macedonia, Greece
Aastha Madaan, University of Southampton, UK
Maria Maleshkova, Karlsruhe Institute of Technology (KIT), Germany
Khalid Mahmood Malik, Oakland University, USA
Zoubir Mammeri, IRIT - Toulouse, France

Yu Suzuki, Nara Institute of Science and Technology, Japan
Sayed Gholam Hassan Tabatabaei, Isfahan University of Technology, Iran
Andon Tchechmedjiev, Laboratoire d'Informatique, Robotique et Microéléctronique de Montpellier (LIRMM) at the University of Montpellier, France
Michele Tomaiuolo, University of Parma, Italy
Orazio Tomarchio, Universita' di Catania, Italy
Vicente Traver, ITACA - Universitat Politècnica de València, Spain
Christos Troussas, University of Piraeus, Greece
Alexander Troussov, Russian Presidential Academy of National Economy and Public Administration, Russia
Žiga Turk, University of Ljubljana, Slovenia
Bert-Jan van Beijnum, University of Twente, The Netherlands
Iván P. Vélez-Ramírez, Axiomática Inc., Puerto Rico
Jian Yu, Auckland University of Technology, New Zealand
Sherali Zeadally, University of Kentucky, USA
Yongfeng Zhang, University of Massachusetts Amherst, USA
Martin Zimmermann, Lucerne University of Applied Sciences and Arts, Switzerland

Copyright Information

Sensor Gateway Using Arduino via Google Cloud and IEEE 802.15.4e

Seung Hyeok, Shin
Dept. of Applied Mathematics, Kumoh National Institute of Technology
51, Daehak-ro, Gumi-si Gyeongsangbuk-do 39177, Korea
shinbaad@kumoh.ac.kr

Lee Sub, Lee
Dept. of Computer Engineering, Kumoh National Institute of Technology
51, Daehak-ro, Gumi-si Gyeongsangbuk-do 39177, Korea
eesub@kumoh.ac.kr

Won Sok, Yoo
Dept. of Applied Mathematics, Kumoh National Institute of Technology
51, Daehak-ro, Gumi-si Gyeongsangbuk-do 39177, Korea
wsyoo@kumoh.ac.kr

***Abstract*—In this paper, we described a sensor gateway for using in a hierarchical network architecture. We propose a gateway architecture termed "Light-Weight Gateway", which provides multiple interfaces to IEEE 802.15.4e called Zigbee and IEEE 802.11 called Wi-Fi, for supporting Google cloud client. For this, we used Arduino as wireless sensor gateway on Google cloud messaging service. It is possible to expose its functionality as an Internet of Things (IoT) node. The Arduino receives sensor information and sends it to the network through Google cloud using Wi-Fi module.**

Keywords-Arduino;Sensor Gateway;Google Cloud Messaging Service;IEEE 802.15.4e;Wireless Seneor Network.

I. Introduction

A Wireless Sensor Network (WSN) is a network consisting of distributed devices that provide sensing features such as industrial gas problems, pipe vibration, noise, motion, etc. Nowadays, WSN systems are developed more and more intelligently. [1]. The Future WSN aims to integrate heterogeneous communication technologies in order to substantially contribute to asserting the concept of IoT. The low cost of sensor technology has eased the proliferation of WSN in many applications, such as real-time monitoring, bio technology, and smart factories [2].

In this paper, we propose a scheme of wireless communication system. This low-cost, small-sized system can collect real-time environmental values, such as gas pressure, stink, noise, humidity and temperature data remotely. Figure 1 shows the overall system architecture.

II. Related Researches

In this section, we introduce google cloud messaging service.

A. *Google Cloud Messaging Service*

Google provides a service called Firebase Cloud Messaging(FCM), which we can be used to send data to the user's device from app server and even receive messages from the devices to our servers through the same connection [3][4]. Figure 1 shows entities in the FCM. It also shows the scenario of FCM client registration and data sending. FCM consists of three parts, FCM client, app server and connection server. Some IDs and tokens used in different stages are described as follows. First, we have to apply an API key from Google, and then get a Sender ID. Registration ID is then issued from the FCM app server to the FCM application that allows it to receive messages. If the FCM device wants to join push group, it sends Sender ID to FCM server and Registration ID to the app server for identifying each device and registering to receive messages for FCM application. When app server wants to push messages, it sends its own API Key and user's Registration ID to FCM server, and then sends messages to FCM server. There are two types of messages in FCM. One is the send-to-sync message, and the other is the message with payload. The send-to-sync message is a light message used in notifying the app on mobile device to update information. On the other hand, the payload message is able to contain up to 4 KB, and is often used to exchange instant messages. The proposed push notification adopts both of two types.

We implemented the cloud messaging system based on FCM service. It consists of four major components: sensor gateway, FCM client as a smart phone application, app server and mongo database as shown in Figure 1.

III. Implementation

In this section, we introduce light weight gateway and proposed architecture.

A. *Light Weight Gateway*

Arduino is an open-source hardware platform. The Arduino Uno is a microcontroller board based on the ATmega328p-pu [5]. The Arduino does not have built-in Wi-Fi and 802.15.4e connectivity. Instead, it is added by connecting Wi-Fi and ZigBee module. Modules are connected to the Arduino using a serial port or an API mode. Also, wireless capabilities are added by forwarding any data received from the 802.15.4e network to the Google cloud and forwarding received Google cloud to the 802.15.4e network, respectively. Figure 2 shows the proposed Arduino gateway.

B. *Proposed Architecture*

The main ingredient for any IoT based operation is a sensor gateway and app server [6]. The centralized sensor gateway acts as the heart of all the IoT rooted operation. In this paper, the app server is used for data storage, sensor feedback and control [7]. A virtual connection between the app server and FCM client devices include sensor gateway that needs to be created. There are several ways to make an Internet connection form, which we have used FCM. Figure 3 shows the proposed system architecture.

Most FCM systems use an external app server to send notifications via the Google cloud. In this paper, we proposed a modified FCM registration about sensor gateway. Therefore, sensor gateway stores the FCM client registration ids. So, sensor gateway can send a sensing data to the FCM client individually.

IV. RESULT

Figure 4 shows the registration sequence. Figure 4(a) is the FCM sequence and 4(b) is the proposed system sequence. Proposed sequence is more complex than FCM sequence. FCM client registration request is occurred twice in proposed sequence. This means that proposed sequence is too complex in the registration sequence. But this sequence is not important in entire FCM sequence, because registration is not being occurred frequently.

Figure 5 shows the push message sequence. Figures 5(a) and 5(b) show FCM sequence and proposed system sequence. FCM sequence is more complex than the proposed sequence. The sensor gateway for push message sequence is used in the proposed sequence. This means that proposed sequence reduced the step of the request data and user account. Since push message sequence is occurring more frequently, it is more efficient than FCM sequence.

Figure 6 shows time complexity graph of Big-O. Figure 6(a) is the registration sequence and 6(b) is the push message sequence. The graph of $y=O(n)$ shows the FCM sequence and $y=O(n^2)$ shows the proposed sequence in Figure 6(a). As shown in the graph, the proposed registration sequence is more complex than FCM sequence. The graph of $y=O(n^{2n})$ shows the proposed sequence and $y=(On^n)$ shows the FCM sequence in Figure 6(b). As shown in the graph, the FCM sequence is more complex than proposed sequence.

V. CONCLUSION

In this paper, we have described how to compose Arduino by adding an 802.15.4e and FCM client function, in order to use it as a sensor gateway. We also modified the registration sequence on Google cloud, and showed efficient push message sequence. We have described all of the necessary steps to make a registration sequence. In addition, we have described the design and implementation of Arduino sensor gateway, which can be used for WSN. To demonstrate the applicability of our system, we have presented two representative scenarios of use cases that illustrate how our infrastructure can be used.

Our future work includes the implementation of additional applications, which is smart phone application and web data visualization system.

REFERENCES

[1] I. Agranat, "Embedded web servers in network devices", Communication Systems Design, Mar. 1998.

[2] P. P. Pereira, J. Eliasson, R. Kyusakov, and M. Johansson, "Enabling Cloud-connectivity for Mobile Internet of Things Applications", IEEE Seventh International Symposium on Service-Oriented System Engineering, 2013, pp. 518-526.

[3] P. Klasnja, and W. Pratt, "Healthcare in the pocket: mapping the space of mobile-phone health interventions," Journal of biomedical informatics, Vol. 45, No. 1, pp. 184–198, 2012.

[4] M. Berglund, C. Nilsson, P. R´evay, G. Petersson, and G. Nilsson, "Nurses and nurse students demands of functions and usability in apda", International Journal of Medical Informatics, Vol. 76, No. 7, pp. 530–537, 2007.

[5] Arduino website, May 2018. [Online]. Available: http://www.arduino.cc/

[6] B. S. Fjeldsoe, A. L. Marshall, and Y. D. Miller, "Behavior change interventions delivered by mobile telephone short-message service", American Journal of Preventive Medicine, Vol. 36, No. 2, pp. 165–173, 2009.

[7] E. S. Bradley, D. A. Roberts, P. E. Dennison, R. O. Green, M. Eastwood, S. R. Lundeen, I. B. McCubbin, and I. Leifer, "Google earth and google fusion tables in support of time-critical collab-oration: Mapping the deep water horizon oil spill with the aviris airborne spectrometer", Earth Sci-ence Informatics, Vol. 4, No. 4, pp. 169–179, 2011.

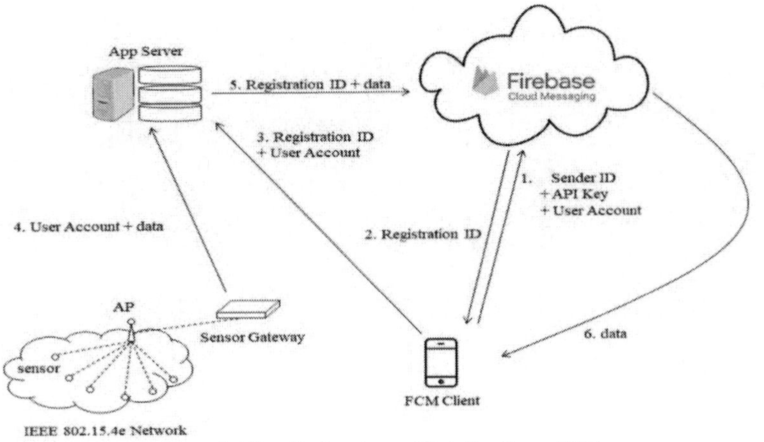

Figure 1. Client Registration and Data Sending on FCM

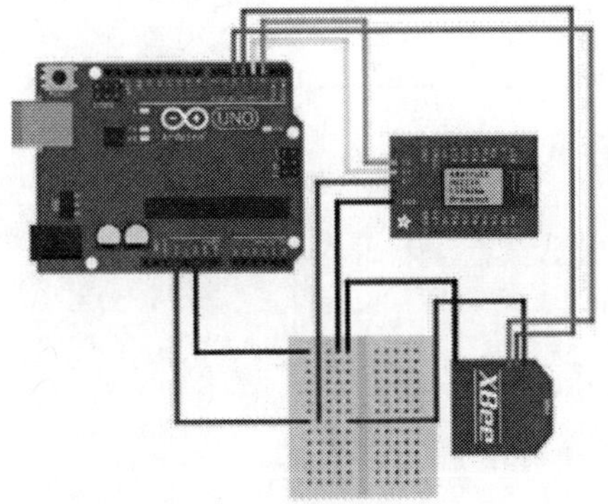

Figure 2. Proposed Sensor Gateway

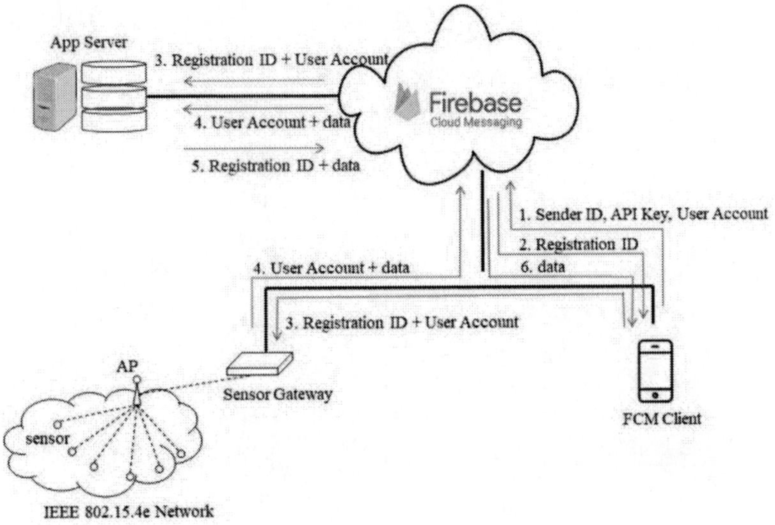

Figure 3. Proposed System Architecture

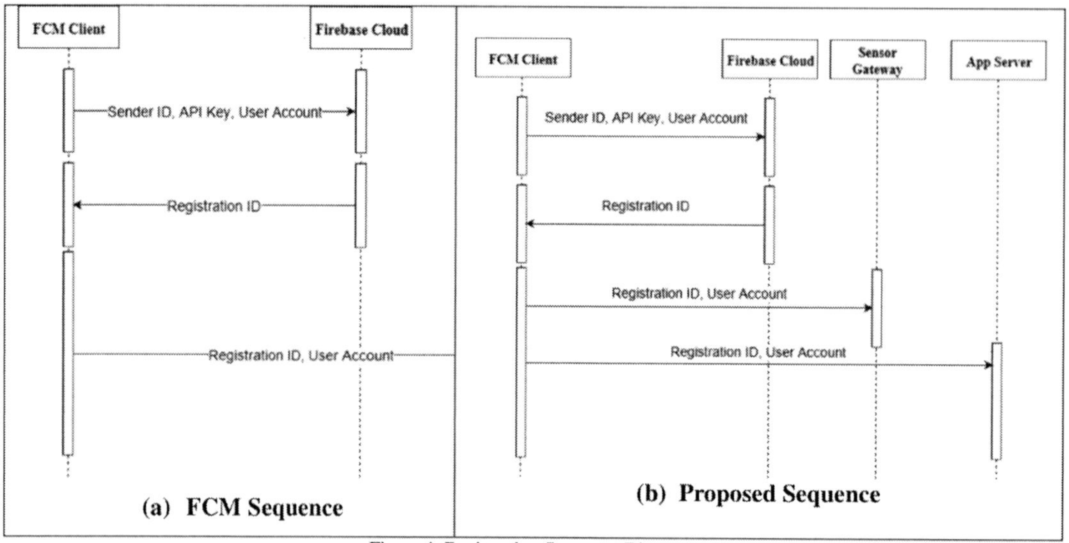

Figure 4. Registration Sequence Diagram

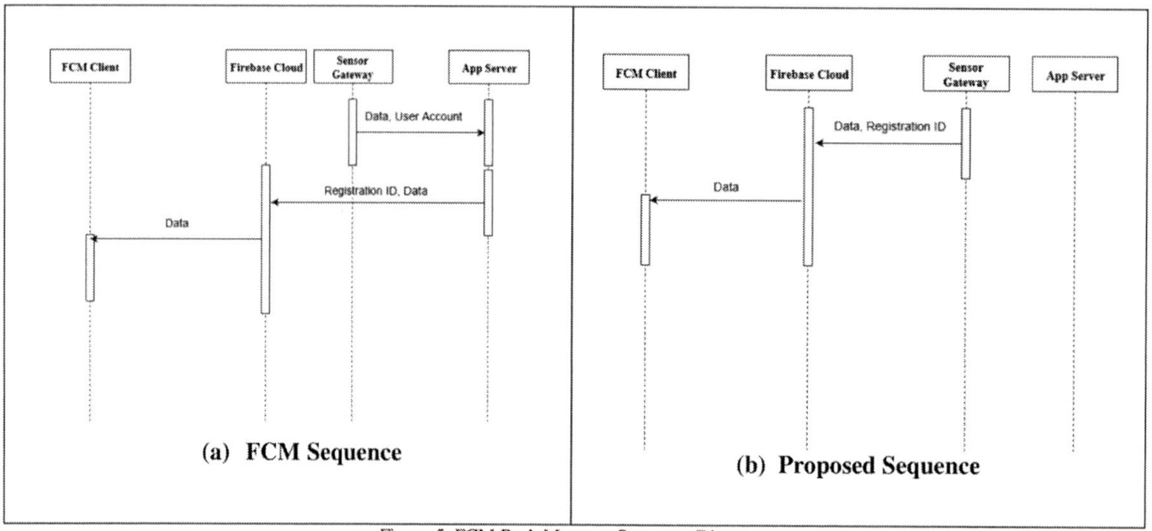

Figure 5. FCM Push Message Sequence Diagram

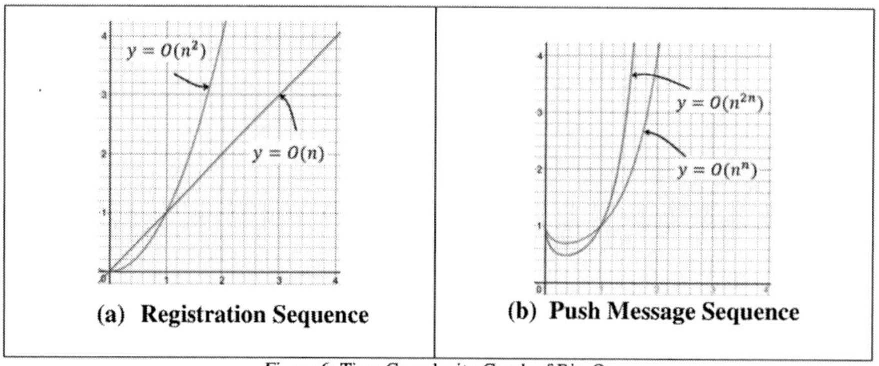

Figure 6. Time Complexity Graph of Big-O

Personalized IaaS Services Selection Based on Multi-Criteria Decision Making Approach and Recommender Systems

Hamdi Gabsi*, Rim Drira†, Henda Hajjami Ben Ghezala‡
RIADI Laboratory. National School of Computer Sciences
University of Manouba,
la Manouba, Tunisia
Email: *hamdi.gabsi@ensi-uma.tn, †rim.drira@ensi-uma.tn, ‡henda.benghezala@ensi-uma.tn

***Abstract*—Cloud computing is becoming tremendously popular owning to its advantages such as elasticity, availability and on demand computing. Actually, the number of cloud providers and their offered services is rapidly growing, in particular for Infrastructures as a Service (IaaS). A huge number of IaaS providers and services is becoming available with different configuration options including pricing policy, storage capacity and computing performance. Therefore, IaaS provider selection and services configuration require a high level of expertise. For these reasons, we aim to assist beginner users in making educated decisions with regard to the technical needs of their application, their preferences and their previous experiences. To do so, we propose a hybrid approach merging both Multi-Criteria Decision Making Methods and Recommender Systems for IaaS provider selection and services configuration. Our solution is implemented in a framework called IaaS Selection Assistant(IaaSSelAss); its effectiveness is demonstrated through an evaluation simulation.**

Keywords- IaaS services selection; Recommender Systems; Multi-Criteria Decision Making;

I. Introduction

Cloud computing is a model for enabling ubiquitous, convenient and on-demand network access to a shared pool of configurable computing resources (e.g., networks, servers, storage, applications and services). These resources can rapidly be provisioned and released with minimal management effort [1]. Particularly, Infrastructure as a Service (IaaS) offers highly scalable resources that can be adjusted on-demand. Due to the increasing number of IaaS providers and their heterogeneity, selecting the appropriate IaaS provider is a challenging task. In fact, each IaaS provider offers a wide range of resources and services which must be appropriately selected and correctly configured. This diversity leaves users in the agony of choice and lead to a steep documentation curve to compare IaaS providers and their services. Thus, it is crucial to assist cloud users during their selection process. In this context, several works such as [2]-[4] have shown an interest to address IaaS selection difficulties. However, these works focused mainly on assisting IaaS services selection based on technical application requirements and Quality of Services (QoS) (which we call application profile). Few studies have highlighted the importance of involving the user in the selection process by taking into account his preferences and his previous experiences (which we call user profile). Consequently, there is a need for a selection process centered on both user and application profiles.

In this paper, we propose a hybrid approach based on Recommender Systems (RS) and Multi-Criteria Decision Making Methods (MCDM). RS are programs which try to recommend suitable items (e.g., movies, music, books and products in general) to a given user by predicting his interest in items [5]-[7]. RS predict and provide relevant recommendations according to user's profile and based on rating given by other similar users profiles. Our solution detailed in this paper for assisting the choice of IaaS providers is based on applying recommendation techniques. Once the IaaS provider is chosen, the user needs to be assisted to handle the services selection and configuration. For us, the cloud services selection is a MCDM problem [3][8][9]. MCDM can be defined as a process for identifying items that match the goals and constraints of decision makers with a finite number of decision criteria and alternatives [9]. In our work, we consider IaaS Service selection as a MCDM problem since users have to make a decision to select a service amongst several candidates services with respect to different criteria. We study and choose the adequate MCDM technique to assist IaaS services selection. So, our approach aims to assist IaaS provider and services selection by involving the user in the selection process and by combining RS and MCDM techniques.

The contributions of this paper can be summarized as follows:

- Defining a classification for relevant criteria that should be used during the selection process. These criteria take into account both applications profile including functional and non functional requirements and user's profile including personal preferences, previous experiences and even lessons learned from experiences of other users.
- Presenting a new hybrid approach based on MCDM and RS techniques for IaaS provider and services selection.

- Implementing this approach in a framework which we term IaaSSelAss for IaaS providers and services selection.

The remainder of this paper is organized as follows: Section 2 summarizes existing IaaS service selection techniques; Section 3 discusses these techniques; Section 4 presents our contributions; Section 5 illustrates an evaluation simulation to showcase the working of our approach and finally Section 6 provides concluding remarks and outlines our ongoing works.

II. Related Work

Our work has taken shape in the context of a rich literature focused on simplifying the IaaS services selection with respect to application requirements. We present a classification of recent research approaches for IaaS services selection inspired from [8].

A. MCDM-based approaches for cloud service selection

Over the years, MCDM has emerged as an important research area having immense practical significance in numerous scientific and engineering problems. This technique can be defined as a process for identifying items that best fit the goals and constraints of decision makers with a finite number of decision criteria and alternatives [8]. The most popular MCDM methods used for cloud service selection are the analytic hierarchy process/analytic network process (AHP/ANP) [10], Multi-Attribute Utility Theory (MAUT) [11], and Simple Additive Weighting (SAW) [8].

Several research studies used MCDM based approaches for cloud service selection. We focused on Zia et al. [9] who propose a methodology for multi-criteria cloud service selection based on cost and performance criteria. The authors present this selection problem in a generalized and abstract mathematical form. Table I illustrates the mathematical form. The service selection process is fundamentally a comparison between the vector service descriptor D against all rows of the decision matrix followed by the selection of the services whose description vector best matches with the user's requirement vector.

B. Recommender systems

RS can be defined as programs which attempt to recommend suitable items to particular users by predicting a user's interest in items based on related information about the items, the users and the interactions between them [5]. Generally, RS use data mining techniques to generate meaningful suggestions taking into account user's preferences. Many different approaches using RS have been developed to deal with the problem of cloud services selection.

Table I. Problem formalization [9]

Mathematical form	Description
Services set	S_1, S_2, ..., S_n A set of services contains all the service offerings from which the user (decision maker) will select the suitable service with regard to his requirements. a service is to be selected by the user (decision maker).
Performance criteria set	C_1, C_2,..., C_n A set of values where C_i represents a criterion that may be a useful parameter for service selection.
Performance measurement functions set	To each criteria C_i there corresponds a unique function f_i which when applied to a particular service, returns a value p_i that is an assessment of its performance on a predefined scale.
Service descriptor (vector)	A row vector D_i that describes a service S_i, where each element d_j of D_i represents the performance or assessment of service S_i under criteria C_j. Performance criteria must be normalized to eliminate computational problems resulting from dissimilarity in measurement units. The normalization procedure is used to obtain dimensionless units that are comparable.
Decision matrix	The service descriptor vectors D_i can be combined to form the decision matrix where each value is the evaluation of the service s_i against the criteria c_j.
User requirement criteria vector	A vector R where each value r_i is the user's minimal requirement against a criteria c_j. These values must be normalized as the vector service descriptor.
User priority weights vector	A vector W where each value w_i is the weight assigned by a user to criteria. c_i

Zhang et al. [6] have offered a cloud recommender system for selecting IaaS services. Based on user's technical requirements, the system recommends suitable cloud services. The matching between technical requirements and cloud services features is based on a cloud ontology. The proposed system uses a visual programming language (widgets) to enable cloud service selection.

Zain et al. [7] propose an unsupervised machine learning technique in order to select cloud services. In fact, the authors classify cloud services into different clusters based on their QoS. The main focus of this study is to offer users the option of choosing a cloud service without engaging into any financial contact. Table II summarizes the most used approaches by identifying the approach's input, the approach's output and the application areas.

The research studies cited previously did not fail to take into consideration the application's functional requirements. Despite the importance of these requirements, we consider

TABLE II. SELECTION APPROACHES

Domain	Method	Input	Output	Application	Literature
Multi-criteria decision-making (MCDM)	SAW	Subjective assessment of relative importance of criteria.	Evaluation value of alternatives.	Applied when requiring low decision accuracy.	[8][9][12]
Multi-criteria optimization	Matrix factorization	Different types of data of interest to users and represented by matrix .	QoS estimation and a set of recommended services.	Applied to a problem that involves different types of data and has missing entries.	[13][14]
Logic based matching approach	First-order logic	Service description and user requirements.	Matched services	Applied to filter out unmatched services to reduce computation complexity.	[8][15]
Recommender System	Collaborative filtering	User's profile	Recommended items	Applied to find personalized recommendations according to user's profile.	[4][6][16]

that this is not enough and users should be more involved in the selection process and hence, their preferences and previous experiences should be taken into account.

To the best of our knowledge, no specific research study has taken into account both the user's profile and the application's requirements. Consequently, there is a need to a structured selection process where clearly both selection criteria are defined and used.

III. HYBRID APPROACH FOR IAAS SERVICES SELECTION BASED ON RS & MCDM

We propose a hybrid approach to assist users in selecting IaaS providers and services based on RS and MCDM. In this section, we start by detailing our selection criteria. Then, we detail our approach.

A. Selection Criteria

In order to recommend the appropriate IaaS services, it is important to specify precise selection criteria. Our purpose is to personalize the selection process according to the user's profile and respond to his application requirements. To this end, we classify our selection criteria into three categories. The first category is the application's profile which includes technical requirements. The second category is the user's profile which represents user's personal preferences and previous experiences. The third category is the previous experiences of other users with their ratings. Figure 1 illustrates our proposed selection criteria. As shown in Figure 1, the selection criteria is classified as the following:

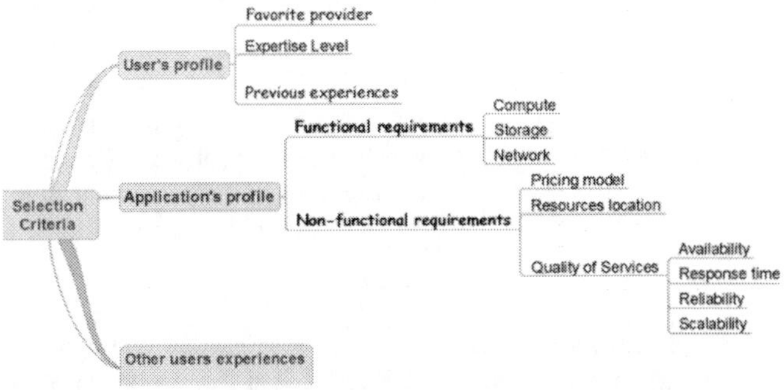

Figure 1. Selection Criteria

- **User's profile:** it includes user's favorite providers, expertise level in cloud and previous experiences. A favorite provider can be chosen based on previous successful experiences using this provider. We take this choice into consideration while identifying the appropriate cloud provider meeting user's requirements. In our case, the user can specify one or multiple favorite providers. The user's expertise level can be: beginner, intermediate or expert. The weight of a user's previous experience in our knowledge base increase with his level of expertise and experience in order to enhance our recommendations relevance A previous experience contains the selected IaaS provider, the deployed application profile and a rating out of 5 presenting a feedback and an evaluation of this experience. We suppose that evaluating ratings are trustworthy and objective.
- **Application's profile:** the application's profile defines the functional and non-functional application requirements.
  Functional requirements are classified into three categories [17].
  - Storage: represents storage needs in terms of memory space.
  - Network: represents connection needs and network usage.
  - Compute: gathers calculation needs and the virtual machine's capacity.

  Non-functional requirements include pricing models, the quality of services (QoS) and the resources location.
  - The pricing model: depends on the user's estimated budget. The pricing model can be on demand, reserved or bidding and can be evaluated per hour or per month.
  - QoS: we focus on the response time, the availability and the reliability. The availability is the time ratio when the service is functional to the total time it is required or expected to function in. The

reliability is represented by the percentage of how long the service can perform its agreed function without interruption.
  - Resources location: The user can precise his nearest resources location because it is important to take into account the proximity when selecting the cloud infrastructure services. According to [15], during the interaction between the users and servers, there is a strong inverse correlation between network distance and bandwidth. Thus, factoring the proximity into the selection of IaaS services can significantly reduce the client's response time and increase the network bandwidth.
- **Previous users experiences:** The more the knowledge base of our recommender system is rich, the more recommendations will be relevant. Therefore, previous users experiences which include deployed application profile, selected IaaS provider and the evaluating rating will improve the accuracy of our recommendations.

B. RS and MCDM based selection approach

The selection of IaaS provider and services configuration is a complex issue. To tackle this issue, we propose a two steps selection process. The first step focuses on selecting the IaaS provider based on the collaborative filtering which is a RS approach. The purpose of this step is to reduce the number of inappropriate IaaS provider which may not interest the user. The second step concerns the configuration of services within the selected provider from the first step. It's based on SAW which is a MCDM method. Our proposed approach shows how MCDM techniques and RS are complementary in order to involve both technical and personal aspects in the selection process.

1) Recommender System: The first step aims to take into consideration the user's preferences, previous experiences and expertise level during the selection process. In our approach, we use the collaborative filtering algorithm also known as k-NN collaborative filtering. This recommendation algorithm bases its predictions on previous users experiences and their profiles. The main assumption behind this method is that other users ratings can be selected and aggregated so that a reasonable prediction of the active user's preferences is deduced.

To recommend the IaaS provider meeting the user's profile we proceed as follows:

- First, we select the users profiles which have the same or higher expertise level than the active user "A". For example, if "A" has the expertise level intermediate, then, from our knowledge base, we select a first list named "list1" of users profiles which are intermediate or expert and their rated experiences.
- Second, among the high rated previous experiences of list1, we select those which are based on the favorite providers of "A" in order to create a second list named "list2".
- Third, among these experiences, "A" can refine list2 by identifying experiences that have similar applications to his application's profile. We obtain list3. Indeed, we aim by these three steps verifying if "A" favorite providers can be suitable for "A" application profile. Otherwise, we skip the second step to apply the third step on list1.
- Then, a rating $R_{(A,f_i)}$ is calculated for each one of candidate providers f_i of list3. $R_{(A,f_i)}$ is calculated as bellow:

$$R_{(A,f_i)} = \frac{\sum_{j=1}^{n} w_{(A,j)}(v_{j,f_i} - \overline{v_j})}{\sum_{j=1}^{n} |w_{(A,j)}|}$$

  where n is the number of identified users' profiles of list3, $w_{(A,j)}$ is the similarity between the profile of "A" and the identified users profiles j of list3, v_{j,f_i} is the rate given by the user j to the provider f_i, $\overline{v_j}$ is the rating's average given by the user j to the favorites providers of "A". We calculate similarity between "A" and the identified users using cosine similarity.

$$w_{(A,j)} = \frac{\sum_{k=1}^{n} v_{A,k} * v_{j,k}}{\sqrt{\sum_{k=1}^{n} v_{A,k}^2 \sum_{k=1}^{n} v_{j,k}^2}},$$

  where the sum on k is the set of providers for which "A" and the selected users in list 3 both assigned a rating, $v_{j,k}$ is the rate given by the user j to the provider k.
- Finally, we propose to "A", the set of providers sorted according to the rate calculated, thus the active user can select one provider.

2) Multi-Criteria Decision Making: Once the IaaS provider is selected, the second step consists on determining suitable IaaS services. In fact, several and conflicting criteria have to be taken into account when making a service selection decision. No single service exceeds all other services in all criteria but each service may be better in terms of some of the criteria. Since users have to decide which service to select amongst several candidates services with respect to different criteria, we consider IaaS Service selection as a MCDM problem. Among MCDM methods, we use the SAW method also known as weighted linear combination or scoring methods. It is based on the weighted average of different criteria. The purpose of using SAW method in our approach is to respond precisely to the application's profile.

The user introduces computing requirements (e.g., virtual Central Processing Unit (vCPU)), storage requirements (e.g., hard drive's size), network requirements (e.g., throughput and bandwidth). The user inserts also the QoS required (e.g., response time and Availability) and the pricing model (e.g., on demand, reserved, bidding).

To be able to apply the SAW algorithm, we need to formalize our decision problem. For that, we define a decision matrix related to the user. In parallel an analogous decision matrix is defined for the IaaS provider selected in the first step. The decision matrix is a combination of service descriptor vectors. Each service descriptor vector represents the performance of a service under a particular criteria. These criteria represent functional and non-functional requirements for the user. For each criterion, the user adds a weight to represent the importance of this criterion. Table III demonstrates an extract form of the decision matrix related to Azure Microsoft [18].

TABLE III. EXTRACT OF DECISION MATRIX FOR MICROSOFT AZURE (VIRTUAL MACHINE)

Service	VCPU	RAM	Hard Drive's size	Cost
A0	1	0,75 GB	19 GB	$0,02/h
A1	1	1,75 GB	224 GB	$0,08/h
A2	2	3,5 GB	489 GB	$0,16/h
A3	4	7 GB	999 GB	$0,32/h
A4	8	14 GB	2039 GB	$0,64/h
A5	2	14 GB	489 GB	$0,35/h
A6	4	28 GB	999 GB	$0,71/h

The SAW algorithm is based on the calculation of one score to each alternative (an alternative in our case is an IaaS service offered by the selected IaaS provider). According to the following SAW formula, the alternative score is calculated as (A_i)=$\sum w_j v_{ij}$, where w_j is the alternative's weight i according to criterion j and v_{ij} its performance. The alternative with the highest score will be suggested. By applying this formula, the recommended IaaS service will automatically be the most performing service, because it has the highest performing values in the decision matrix (highest number of vCPU, largest hard drive's size, highest cost, etc.). However, this does not entirely meet the user's requirements, because, he/she must not necessarily select the most performing IaaS service which will evidently have the highest cost. Whereas, he/she should select the service which meets exactly his/her requirements in order to pay the minimum possible cost. To solve this, we proceed as follows:

- First, we create the decision matrix representing the application's profile by gathering user's functional and non-functional requirements. Then, we determine for each service descriptor vector, the absolute value of the difference between its criteria performance and those of the service descriptor vector related to the IaaS provider. In this way, we will have significant values. In fact, low criteria values mean that they accurately match the user's requirements.
- Second, we calculate the score for each alternative using SAW algorithm. Yet, to be able to do so, we need to modify each criterion's weight to get significant results. Indeed, we have previously mentioned that a low criterion's value means that it may interest the user, if this criterion has a high weight, the multiplication of its weight by its value gives a low score. Therefore, this alternative will be considered as unimportant, yet this is not the case. To solve this problem we take the dual of each weight, meaning that, the subtraction of 1 by the weight's value given by the user. The weight values are between 0 and 1. Consequently, one low weight value indicates a major importance of a given criterion. Thus, we can calculate the score for each alternative using the SAW algorithm. The most relevant alternative (IaaS service) will incontrovertibly have the lowest score.

To illustrate this, we propose our personalized SAW Algorithm 1. We suppose that the cloud user has introduced his decision matrix $UserMat[i][j]$ as well as the weights of each criterion $Weight[j]$. In addition, we suppose that we have the decision matrix $ProvMat[i][j]$ containing IaaS services offered by the IaaS provider. In the decision matrix $UserMat$, $UserMat[i][j]$ represent the IaaS service i under the criterion j.

$$UserMat = \begin{bmatrix} u_{00} & \cdots & u_{0n} \\ \vdots & \ddots & \vdots \\ u_{n0} & \cdots & u_{nm} \end{bmatrix}$$

Our personalized SAW algorithm gives as output, the index i representing the adequate cloud service i in the decision matrix.

Algorithm 1 Personalized SAW Algorithm

Require: $Weight[i] \neq 0$
  $Min = 0$
  for $int\ i\ from\ 0\ to\ n$ **do**
    for $int\ j\ from\ 0\ to\ n$ **do**
      $Sub[i][j] = abs(ProvMat[i][j] - UserMat[i][j])$
    end for
  end for
  for $int\ j\ from\ 0\ to\ m$ **do**
    $DualWeight[j] = 1 - Weight[j]$
  end for
  for $int\ i\ from\ 0\ to\ n$ **do**
    $Score[i] = 0$
    for $int\ j\ from\ 0\ to\ m$ **do**
      $Score[i] = Score[i] + Sub[i][j] * DualWeight[j]$
    end for
  end for
  for $int\ i\ from\ 0\ to\ n$ **do**
    if $Score[i] < Min$ **then**
      $Min \leftarrow Score[i]$
      $Index \leftarrow i$
    end if
  end for
  return i

IV. IaaSSelAss: A Framework for IaaS Selection Assistant

In order to implement our proposed approach, we develop the framework IaaSSelAss. We have used Eclipse Modeling Framework, Java Platform Enterprise Edition (JEE) and Mahout eclipse framework [19]. IaaSSelAss guides cloud users step by step in the selection process and proposes IaaS providers and services with adequacy percentage according to applications and users profile. IaaSSelAss has been designed to support different IaaS providers such as Amazon, Google and Azure Microsoft. We demonstrate the effectiveness of our framework through an evaluation simulation.

The idea of merging RS and MCDM techniques in a structured approach based on two well defined steps as explained in Section IV, provides satisfactory results. In this section, we conduct simulations on 25 real users some of them are PhD students. These simulations show that our approach prove to be efficient rather than using RS and MCDM techniques each independently. We define the simulations' conditions as follows:

- Supported IaaS provider: Amazon, Google, Microsoft Azure
- Number of users: 25
- Number of items (IaaS services): 30
- Active user's profile: User profile 2 defined in Table IV
- Active user's application profile: Active user application profile 2 defined in Table IV
- The non-functional requirements are defined as follows:
  - Pricing model: Per hour
  - Resource Location: US

We define in Table V the decision matrix " $ProvMat[][]$ " used by the personalized SAW algorithm of our approach. Table V contains 5 configuration models of Virtual Machines instances provided by Amazon [20]. Each value in Table V is verified and identified from cloud provider's official web site. Although the number of users and items is relatively small compared to commercial RS, it proves to be sufficient for the purpose of these simulations.

To compare our framework IaaSSelAss to RS techniques (CF algorithm), we omit the step two of our approach, which is the use of personalized SAW algorithm and we rely only on the Collaborative Filtering algorithm in order to create a simple recommender System. The metrics used to evaluate our approach with the use of Rs are the Root-Mean Square Error (RMSE) and The Normalized Discounted Cumulative Gain (NDCG).

The RMSE is a metric widely used to evaluate predicted ratings [21]. It represents the sample standard deviation of the differences between predicted values and expected values. RMSE is the square root of the average of squared errors.

$$RMSE = \frac{\sqrt{\sum_{i=1}^{n}(p_{A,i} - \widehat{p}_{A,i})^2}}{N}$$

where $p_(A,i)$ is a predicted value by user "A" for item i, $\widehat{p}_{A,i}$ is the expected value of user "A" for item i, and N is the number of predicted values. In order to be able to calculate RMSE values, we assume that users introduce their expected rating values.

The Normalized Discounted Cumulative Gain (NDCG) is a measure of ranking quality. NDCG is defined as

$$NDCG_N = \frac{DCG_N}{IDCG_N}$$

where DCG_N and $IDCG_N$ are the Discounted Cumulative Gain (DCG) of top-N items of a predicted ranking and the ideal ranking, respectively. DCG_N is calculated by

$$DCG_N = \sum_{i=1}^{N} \frac{2^{(rel_i)} - 1}{log_2(i+1)}$$

where rel_i is the value of the item at position i of a ranking and $IDCG_N$ is calculated by

$$IDCG_N = \sum_{i=1}^{REL} \frac{2^{(rel_i)} - 1}{log_2(i+1)}$$

where REL represents the list of relevant items (ratings $\geq 0,5$). The value of NDCG is between 0 and 1, where a larger value means a better ranking, and 1 implies the ideal ranking.

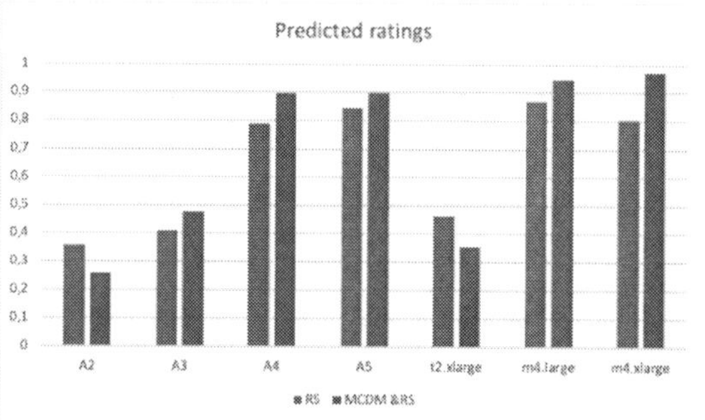

Figure 2. Predicted Ratings

As illustrated in Figure 2 for user 2, the predicted ratings are 0,8403, 0,8053, 0,7872, respectively for AWS instances m4.large, m4.xlarge presented in Table III, and Azure instance A4 presented in Table V. For clarity and visibility purposes, we did not display all instances' predicted ratings of Tables III and V. The scores given by the personalized SAW algorithm of our approach for the same instances are respectively 0,9476, 0,9734, 0,8954. When conducting the CF approach, we obtained 0,042 and 0,571 as RMSE and NDCG average, respectively. However, the RS & MCDM approach gave us 0,031 and 0,73 as RMSE and NDCG

TABLE IV. USERS AND APPLICATIONS PROFILES

User	User profile			Application profile									
	Favorite provider	Expertise level	Previous experi-ences	Functional requirements								QoS	
				Compute			Storage		Network			Response time ms	Avail-ability
				vCPU	Clock speed GHz	CPU events/s	RAM GB	Hard drive's size GB	Bandwidth $\mathrm{Gbit\,s^{-1}}$	Throughput $\mathrm{Mbit\,s^{-1}}$	Latency ms		
Weights User1	-	-	-	0,5	0,3	0,1	0,4	0,6	0,6	0,1	0,3	0,5	0,3
Values User1	-	Beginner	-	2	2	$v \geq 50$	$v \geq 2$	> 50	1	$10 < v \leq 50$	-	$100 < v \leq 900$	95%
Weights User2	-	-	-	0,4	0,2	0,4	0,6	0,4	0,5	0,3	0,2	0,7	0,2
Values User2	Amazon	Intermediate	2	4	3	47	8	80	2	35	70	700	99%

TABLE V. AMAZON DECISION MATRIX [20]

Model	vCPU	Clock speed GHz	CPU events/s	RAM GB	Hard drive GB	Bandwidth $\mathrm{Gbit\,s^{-1}}$	Throughput $\mathrm{Mbit\,s^{-1}}$	Latency ms	Response time ms	Availability
t2.nano	1	3,3	37	0,5	8	-	-	200	1600	99%
t2.medium	2	3,3	42	4	≥ 30	-	-	200	1600	99%
t2.xlarge	4	3,3	42	6	≥ 100	0,7	45	120	1000	99%
m4.large	4	2,4	57	8	≥ 500	1	62	100	700	99%
m4.xlarge	8	2,4	57	16	-	2	125	100	700	99%

average (Figure 3). So, in terms of RMSE (i.e., 0,042 vs.0,031), the merging of MCDM & RS performs better than RS only. In terms of NDCG (i.e., 0,571 vs. 0,73), RS & MCDM present better result than the CF approach.

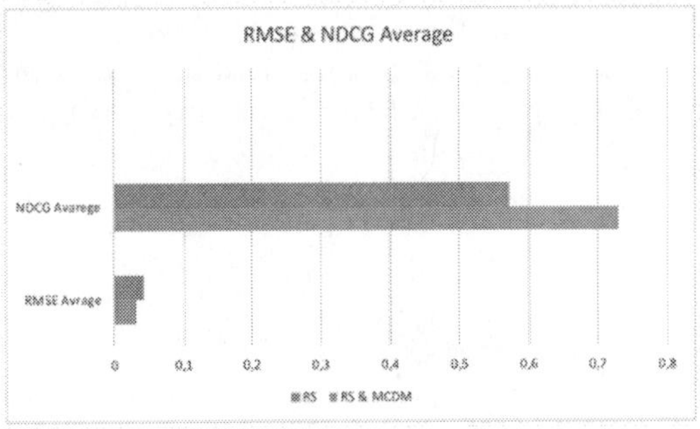

Figure 3. RMSE & NDCG Average

It is worth pointing that the use of CF algorithm only obliges us to calculate predicted ratings for all items in our knowledge base which can be time consuming. However, by applying the step one of our approach we can reduce the number of candidate services by providing only services related to the selected IaaS provider. In addition, the selection of IaaS services using CF algorithm will be associated with previous users experiences in our knowledge base. Although, we identify the most similar users their application profiles must be more or less different to the active user application profile. Consequently, the predicted IaaS services are less accurate. In conclusion, this simulation shows that our approach performs better than using RS only.

V. CONCLUSION

This paper investigates the challenges of selecting appropriate cloud infrastructure and services. We proposed a new hybrid approach that transforms the IaaS services selection from an ad-hoc task that involves manually reading the provider documentations to a structured and guided process. Our solution aims to involve users in the selection process and takes into consideration their personal preferences and their previous experiences in addition to the functional requirements of their applications. Thus, our approach proposes relevant IaaS services responding users expectations. Although we believe that the framework IaaSSelAss supporting our approach leaves scope for a range of enhancements, yet it provides suitable results. For our ongoing works, we are focusing on reducing the complexity of introducing the application's profile, such as CPU clock speed, throughput, etc. In fact, we aim to deduce these requirements from real-world scenarios and experiences, such as the capacity of a server to respond to a given number of users per hour with a required latency between request and response. In addition, we are working on integrating other cloud service models like Platform as a Service(PaaS) or Software as a Service (SaaS). In our approach, we select IaaS services according to a single selected provider, thus, we can extend it to support a Multi-cloud services selection.

REFERENCES

[1] P. Mel and T. Grance, "The nist definition of cloud computing," *NIST Special Publication*, pp. 800–145, 2011, Available at: http://csrc.nist.gov/publications/nistpubs/800-145/SP800-145.pdf [accessed: 2018-05-23].

[2] M. Eisa, M. Younas, K. Basu, and H. Zhu, "Trends and directions in cloud service selection," *IEEE Symposium on Service-Oriented System Engineering*, 2016, ISBN: 978-1-5090-2253-3.

[3] A. J. Ruby, B. W. Aisha, and C. P. Subash, "Comparison of multi criteria decision making algorithms for ranking cloud renderfarm services," *Indian Journal of Science and Technology*, vol. 9, p. 31, 2016.

[4] S. Soltani, K. Elgazzar, and P. Martin, "Quaram service recommender: a platform for iaas service selection," *International Conference on Utility and Cloud Computing*, pp. 422–425, 2016, ISBN: 978-1-4503-4616-0.

[5] J. Lu, D. Wu, and G. Zhang, "Recommender system application developments: A survey," *Decision Support Systems*, vol. 74, pp. 12–32, 2015.

[6] M. Zhang, R. Ranjan, S. Nepal, M. Menzel, and A. Haller, "A declarative recommender system for cloud infrastructure services selection," *GECON*, vol. 7714, pp. 102–113, 2012.

[7] T. Zain, M. Aslam, M. Imran, and Martinez-Enriquez, "Cloud service recommender system using clustering," *Electrical Engineering, Computing Science and Automatic Control (CCE)*, vol. 47, pp. 777–780, 2014.

[8] L. Sun, H. Dong, F. Khadeer, Hussain, O. K. Hussain, and E. Chang, "Cloud service selection: State-of-the-art and future research directions," *Journal of Network and Computer Applications*, vol. 45, pp. 134–150, 2014.

[9] Z. Rehman, F. Hussain, and O. Hussain, "Towards multi-criteria cloud service selection," *International Conference on Innovative Mobile and Internet Services in Ubiquitous Computing*, 2012, ISBN: 978-1-61284-733-7.

[10] C. JatothG and U. Fiore, "Evaluating the efficiency of cloud services using modified data envelopment analysis and modified super-efficiency data envelopment analysis," *Soft Computing, Springer-Verlag Berlin Heidelberg*, vol. 7221-7234, p. 21, 2017.

[11] F. Aqlan, A. Ahmed, O. Ashour, A. Shamsan, and M. M. Hamasha, "An approach for rush order acceptance decisions using simulation and multi-attribute utility theory," *European Journal of Industrial Engineering,*, 2017, ISSN: 1751-5254.

[12] M. Whaiduzzaman, A. Gani, N. B. Anuar, M. Shiraz, M. N. Haque, and I. T. Haque, "Cloud service selection using multicriteria decision analysis," *The Scientific World Journal*, vol. 2014, p. 10, 2014.

[13] L. D. Ngan and R. Kanagasabai, "Owl-s based semantic cloud service broker," *International conference on web services (ICWS)*, pp. 560–567, 2013, ISBN: 978-1-4673-2131-0.

[14] F. K. Hussain, Z. ur Rehman, and O. K. Hussain, "Multi-criteria iaas service selection based on qos history," *International Conference on Advanced Information Networking and Applications*, 2014, ISSN: 1550-445X.

[15] Z. Li, L. OBrien, H. Zhang, and R. Cai, "On the conceptualization of performance evaluation of iaas services," *IEEE Transactions on Services Computing*, vol. 7, pp. 628 – 641, 2014.

[16] Q. Yu, "Cloudrec: a framework for personalized service recommendation in the cloud," *Knowledge and Information Systems*, vol. 43, pp. 417–443, 2014.

[17] C. Qu and R. Buyya, "Oa cloud trust evaluation system using hierarchical fuzzy inference system for service selection," *International Conference on Advanced Information Networking and Applications*, 2014, ISBN: 978-1-4799-3630-4.

[18] "Microsoft Azure," 2018, URL: https://azure.microsoft.com/en-us/pricing/details/cloud-services [accessed: 2018-05-23].

[19] "Mahout Apache," 2018, URL: http://mahout.apache.org/ [accessed: 2018-05-23].

[20] "Amazon Instance Types," 2018, URL: https://aws.amazon.com/ec2/instance-types/?nc1=h_ls [accessed: 2018-05-23].

[21] Z. Zheng, X. Wu, Y. Zhang, M. R.lyu, and J. Wang, "Qos ranking prediction for cloud services," *European Journal of Industrial Engineering,*, vol. 24, pp. 1213–1222, 2013.

Requirement Analysis and Extending CSS3 Specification for Polar Coordinate Text Layout in Web Documents

Soon-Bum Lim, Seung-Min Shim
Dept. of IT engineering
Sookmyung Women's University
Yongsan-gu, Seoul, Korea
e-mail sblim@sm.ac.kr, undervine@naver.com

Abstract— **This study extends the Cascading Style Sheet (CSS) specification in order to place the text along circles or circular sectors in web documents with CSS3 stylesheet. We propose a fan-shaped layout model and define the text layout specifications that are not in the conventional Cartesian coordinates system but in the polar coordinate system, and checked the conformity of the proposed extension specification by implementing the preprocessor that allows checking out the sample contents created by the extended CSS3 specification in the existing web browser.**

Keywords-polar-coordinate; text layout; fan model; HTML; CSS3 stylesheet.

I. INTRODUCTION

With the recent introduction of various devices with round displays, the need for circular text arrangement is increasing. Furthermore, with the advent of the age of big data, the demand of circular arrangement of information is on the rise as the data visualization field is getting attention. Also, we often see examples of text arranged in a circle or curve on logos, posters and publications in everyday life.

However, the existing web standards such as Cascading Style Sheet (CSS) and Scalable Vector Graphics (SVG), which are based on Cartesian coordinate system, are very inconvenient when placing polar-coordinate system text, since you have to separate all the letters from the text and set the coordinates of the individual letters in order to place it. Thus, a concise and standardized approach is needed to handle various cases of polar-coordinate text layout.

There was a study how to determine automatic character arrangement and orientation when placing text vertically in the existing CSS specification which became the standard module of CSS3 writing-mode [1]. New CSS3 modules of round displayed text for circular display devices [2] and 3D stereoscopic contents [3] were proposed, but the layout concept was not generalized to place any text in polar-coordinated space.

We analyzed related works in Section 2, and case studies and user requirements in Section 3. Then, we proposed a fan model and extend the CSS3 specification for the various types of text layout in polar coordinate system in Section 4. In Section 5, we checked the feasibility of the extended specification by implementing a preprocessor in the existing web browser. And we described the conclusions in Section 6.

II. RELATED WORK

In the previous CSS standard, Elika J. Etemad researched an automated arrangement and orientation method for situations where there are multiple characters with different typesetting in a vertical layout [1], which became the standard module of CSS3 Writing-mode. This study shows how a CSS standard is designed: firstly, the text layout styles of different cultures are researched and the user's needs are analyzed; then the needed concept for text layout is modeled by referencing terms from the previous vertical layout; and finally, the CSS standard is expanded.

Furthermore, there is a study of expanding the CSS standard: CSS Extensions for a Round Display [2]. This study consists of multiple proposals for supporting web-based platform devices with circular display, such as a method to detect the circular screen and drawing an outline along the edge, a method to place the contents right inside of the edge, and a method to draw the outline without breaking while the contents is being rendered on the screen. As shown in Fig. 1, polar properties, such as polar-angle, polar-distance, and position, are extended, in order to use the polar coordinate for contents layout.

III. REQUIREMENT ANALYSIS OF POLAR COORDINATE TEXT LAYOUT

In order to design a standard for implementation of polar coordinate text layout on the web, various previous cases of layout were studied, then the user's need was analyzed.

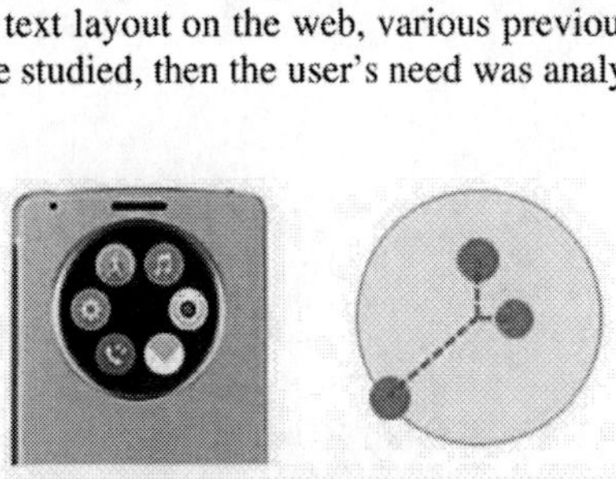

```
<body style="position: polar;">
  <div id="circle1" style="polar-angle: 0deg; polar-distance: 20%"></div>
  <div id="circle2" style="polar-angle: 90deg; polar-distance: 50%"></div>
  <div id="circle3" style="polar-angle: 225deg; polar-distance: 100%"></div>
</body>
```

Figure 1. Examples of polar coordinate layout on the round display.

A. *Case Studies of Polar Coordinate Text Layout*

In the existing cases of polar coordinate text layout, there were some needs of paragraph layout, while most were a single line text layout. Fig. 2(a) shows a case of paragraph layout in polar coordinate.

Furthermore, the direction of text layout appeared differently in polar coordinate. There were both cases where the sentences flowed in clockwise and counter-clockwise, and similar cases with inward and outward. Also, there were few cases where the character orientation was changed, instead of sentences or paragraphs, like shown in Fig. 2(b)

It turned out that a single line sentences were mostly in horizontal writing. However, in data visualizations or infographics, vertical writing was often applied to show a repeated list of data, despite the text being in a single line. Also, in vertical writing, sentences flow to inward or outward, while paragraphs were placed in clockwise or counter-clockwise direction. By contrast, in vertical writing, there were some cases of varying text orientation, as shown in Fig. 2(c), unlike in horizontal writing. .

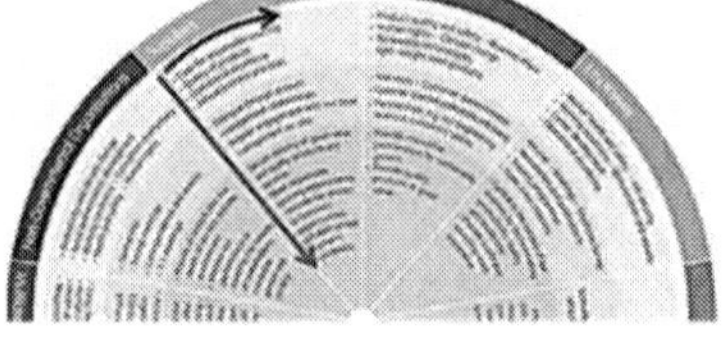

(a) Cases of polar text paragraphs.

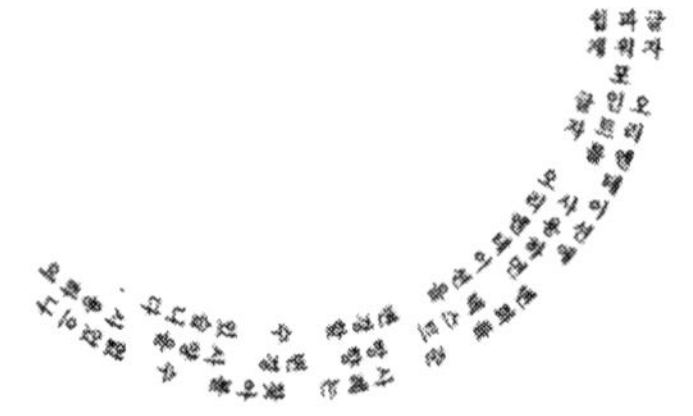

(b) Case of changing text orientations in horizontal writing

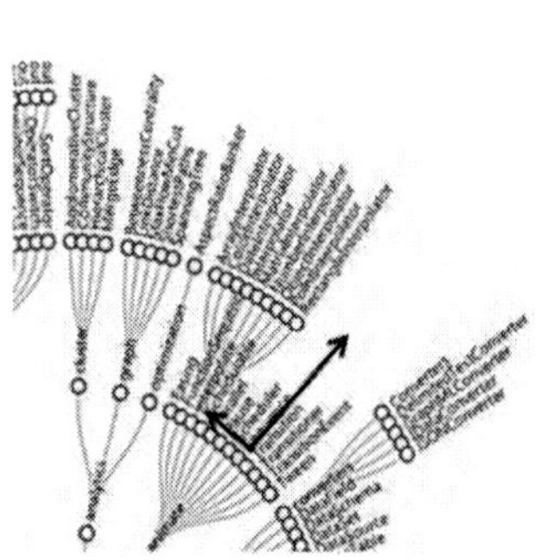

(c) Case of changing text orientation in vertical writing

Figure 2. Case studies of polar coordinate text layout

B. *Requirement Analysis*

As discussed above, in the practical cases of polar coordinate text layout, there are more varying cases than what is possible with the traditional layout. By analyzing the requirements for polar coordinate text layout, it turns out that these points have to be defined in order to place text in polar coordinate.

(1) Text Placement Area

A format model for the area in which the text block is to be placed in the polar coordinate system is needed. In the existing CSS Visual Formatting Model [4], the CSS box model is presented. However, in order to arrange text in the polar coordinate system, an area setting method for a fan-shaped layout model must be prepared.

(2) Sentence and Paragraph Layout

As a result of case studies indicated a high demand for placement of both individual sentences and paragraphs. Like the Cartesian coordinate system, the polar coordinate system requires two types of display: inline and block; see Fig. 3(a).

(3) Placing Text in Various Directions

In the Cartesian coordinate system, there are two types of sentence direction: right and left. In case of paragraph direction, horizontal text always flows from top to bottom, and vertical text flows from left to right. Directionality in the polar coordinate system is more variable and flexible than in the Cartesian coordinate system, and thus a new model is required for polar coordinate system text directionality; see Fig. 3(b).

(4) Placing Text in Vertical Writing

Compared to that of the Cartesian coordinate system, orientations in the polar coordinate system are more variable. According to the CSS3 Writing-mode module, in the Cartesian coordinate system, the sentence directions are either left to right or right to left, and the paragraph directions are always top to bottom for horizontal writing, and either left to right or right to left for vertical writing. Furthermore, the text orientation is limited to top, left, or right. However, in the polar coordinate system, the text could be flipped, or have a varying orientation depending on the degree within the coordinate. Therefore, orientation in the polar coordinate system is more complex than that of the Cartesian coordinate, thus text orientations should be modeled accordingly; see Fig. 3(c).

(5) Placing Text in Different Coordinate Systems in the Same Area

Since general documents assume the use of the Cartesian coordinate system, the polar coordinate system element is located in the Cartesian coordinate system. Conversely, in the case of Fig. 3(d), the Cartesian coordinate system is located within the polar coordinate system. As in this case, it is necessary to define a standard for element arrangement when the two coordinate systems are mixed.

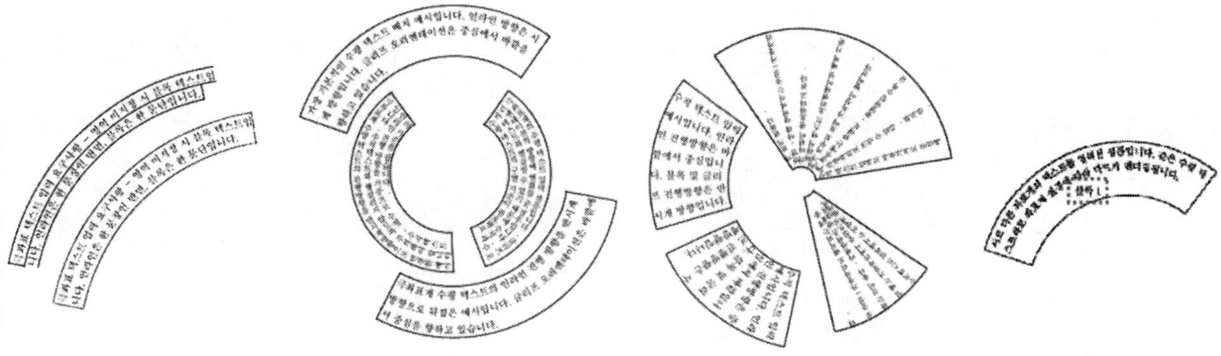

(a) Examples of paragraph layout (b) Examples of various directions (c) Text layout in vertical directions (d) Mixed coordinate system

Figure 3. Examples for requirement analysis

IV. Extended CSS Specification for Polar-Coordinate Text Layout

In the existing CSS, all HTML elements are placed in a rectangular area, in a so-called the box model. In this paper, we propose a fan shaped layout model in polar-coordinate system as shown in Fig. 4, which is called a fan model. According to the CSS visual style model definition [4], the box layout following the CSS box model [5] is defined by box type, box area, position method etc. Likewise, we designed the fan model to be described with fan type, fan area, and position type.

The types of the fan model are divided into fan-block and fan-inline that correspond to block and inline elements of the box model. The positioning method uses the position attribute same as in the box model, because the fan model also specifies the element positioning within the Cartesian coordinate system. The difference is that the box area is placed based on its left-top corner, while the fan area is placed from a reference point, which is the center of the fan shape. Fig. 4 shows the detail attributes of the fan model.

The CSS3 writing-mode module has properties that describe the inline direction, the block direction, and the glyph orientation. While box model has left to right (ltr), right to left (rtl), and top to bottom (tb) directions, the fan model has directions of clockwise (cw), counter-clockwise (ccw), outward to inward (inward), and inward to outward (outward). Therefore, the horizontal writing and vertical writing in fan model can be described as in Fig. 5.

As shown in Table 1, the fan-shape layout specification is divided into three parts: fan model setting, direction setting, and typographic setting, where the prefix '-fan-' is used to distinguish extended attributes. The basic information for the fan model setting is display type, width, and height. The direction setting attributes include sentence direction, paragraph direction, and text orientation. The typographic setting attributes contain indentation, spacing, horizontal alignment and vertical alignment.

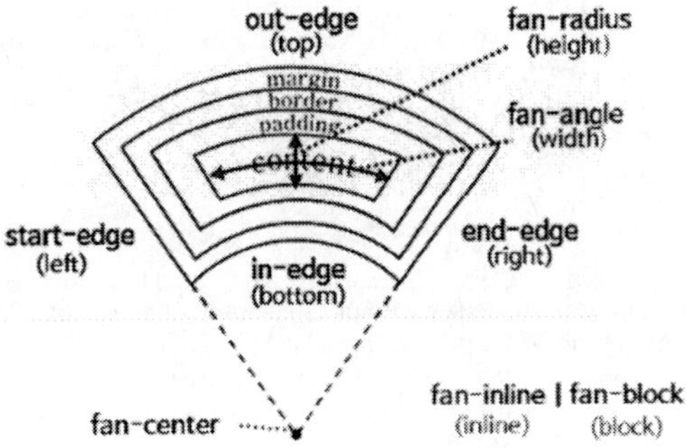

Figure 4. Definition of the fan model

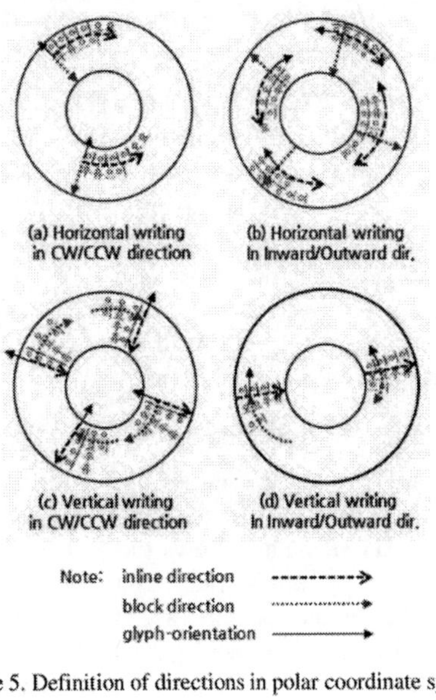

Figure 5. Definition of directions in polar coordinate system

TABLE 1: SPECIFICATION OF CSS3 FAN SHAPE LAYOUT

Category		Extended CSS Specifications
Fan Model Setting	display type	`display : -fan-inline	-fan-block`
	width	`-fan-angle : <angle>	auto`
	height	`-fan-radius : <number>	auto`
Direction Setting	sentence direction	`-fan-direction : cw	ccw	v-inward	v-outward`
	paragraph direction	`-fan-writing-mode : horizontal-auto	v-cw	v-ccw`
	text orientation direction	`-fan-text-orientation : upright	sideways-cw	sideways-ccw	sideways`
Typesetting Properties	indentation	`-fan-indent : <length>`
	alignment	`-fan-align : start-edge	end-edge	center`
	white-spacing	`-fan-white-space : normal	pre-wrap	pre-line`
	vertical-alignment	`-fan-vertical-align: <length>	<percentage>	baseline	sub	super	text-top	text-bottom`

V. FEASIBILITY TEST

Since the proposed CSS3 extension is not working in the current web browser, we developed a preprocessor [6] to translate the extended CSS3 specification into the current CSS3 properties. Using the preprocessor, we evaluated the feasibility of the CSS3 fan model specification whether the extension can efficiently represent the polar-coordinate system text.

For the feasibility test, we developed PowerPoint sample contents that can cover the various cases of polar coordinated text layout as in Fig. 6. Then we compared the results from the code described with our CSS3 fan model with the results from the code using JavaScript library CssWarp.js [7]. From the results, we found out that the results from our CSS3 extension were the same as PowerPoint results, but some of them were not able to be represented with the CssWarp.js library(⑤⑥ in Fig. 6).

Also, we counted the number of tokens in the sample codes, and compared those written in CssWraps.js and CSS3 fan model. While the average number of codes in CssWraps was 78.0, the average in CSS3 fan model was 20.5 where the reduction rate is 26.3%. Therefore, we assessed that we could express the user requirements for polar-coordinate text layout well by using the CSS3 fan model specification proposed in this study.

VI. CONCLUSION AND FUTURE WORK

In this study, we proposed a CSS3 extension in order to place text in a polar-coordinate system in web documents expressed in HTML. This allows the text to be placed in a polar-coordinate system by only using the CSS3 stylesheet in the HTML standard documents. The proposed CSS3 fan model can place sentence and paragraphs, text in multiple directions, and vertical text in polar-coordinate system.

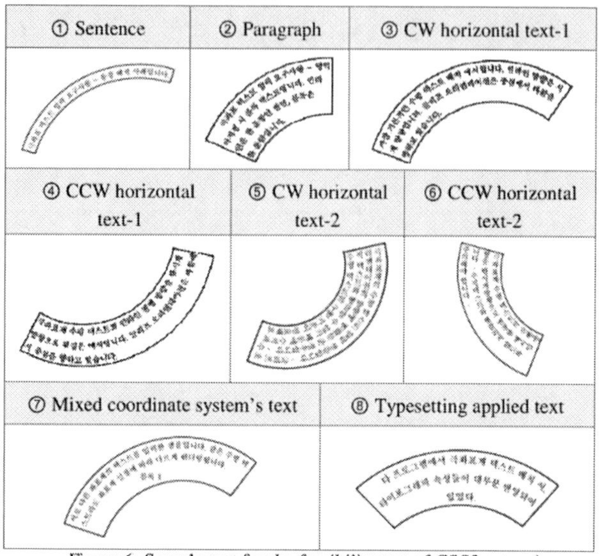

Figure 6. Sample text for the feasibility test of CSS3 extension

The future plan is to implement the extended CSS3 module as a Javascript library to be easily imported by general users, and to standardize it as a regular W3C CSS3 specification module so as to be implemented eventually within the existing web browsers.

ACKNOWLEDGMENT

This work was supported by Institute for Information & communications Technology Promotion (IITP) grant funded by the Korea government (MSIP) (No. 2016-0-00166)

REFERENCES

[1] E. J. Etemad, "Robust vertical text layout," The 27th Internationalization & Unicode Conference, 2005, pp. 15-16.

[2] S. Han, H. Song, and J. Hong, "CSS Round Display Level 1," W3C WD 22, Dec. 2016. [Online] Available from: http://www.w3.org/TR/css-round-display-1/ (accessed 10 April 2018)

[3] S.B. Lim, H.J. Lee, W.Y. Jin, and S.M. Shim, "CSS3 extensions for setting web content in a 3D view volume and its stereoscopic 3D display," Computer Standards & Interfaces. vol.50, pp. 65–75, Feb. 2017.

[4] B. Bos, T. Celik, I. Hickson, and H. Lie, "Cascading Style Sheets Level 2 (CSS 2.1) Specification-9 Visual formatting model," W3C Recommendation, June 2011, [Online] Available from: http://www.w3.org/TR/CSS21/visuren.html (accessed 10 April 2018)

[5] B. Bos, "CSS basic box model," W3C Working Draft, 9 August 2007, [Online] Available from: http://www.w3.org/TR/css3-box/ (accessed 10 April 2018)

[6] S.M. Shim, "CSS3 Extension for Polar-Coordinate Text Layout and its Preprocessor,". Master Thesis. (in Korean) Sookmyung Women's University, Feb. 2016

[7] D. Weber, "CSSWARP, CSS Text to Path Generator," 2011 [Online] Available from: http://csswarp.eleqtriq.com/ (accessed 10 April 2018)

Conformance Checking of IFC Models with the Extensions in the MvdXML Checker

Muhammad Fahad+, Nicolas Bus*
+Experis / ELAN IT
1240 Route des Dolines,
Valbonne 06560, France
email: {firstname.lastname}@experis-it.fr

Bruno Fies*, Franck Andrieux*
*Centre Scientifique et Technique du Bâtiment
290 Route des Lucioles,
Sophia Antipolis 06904, France
email: {firstname.lastname}@cstb.fr

Abstract— **Building codes and standards are the rules and guidelines that specify the minimum acceptable level of safety for buildings. MvdXML Checker is a building code checker for the automatic verification of IFC models and to detect the non-conformities with the associated 3D visualization. The verification approach is based on MvdXML rules to be used within the MvdXML Checker or IfcDoc tool developed by the buildingSMART International to improve the consistent and computer-interpretable definition of Model View Definitions. In this paper, we propose many extensions in the MvdXML Checker which are very useful for the verification of IFC models and discuss its implement as a web service. After these extensions, still we analyze that this traditional approach of verification by the use of MvdXML is very limited and has narrow scope for the verification of IFC models. Major limitations are identified such as restricted scope of applying conditions and constraints on several branches of an IFC model, poor geometric analysis of an IFC model, lack of mathematical calculations, support of only static verification of a model, etc. Therefore, finally we present a need of an approach based on Semantic Web technologies that can easily be extended, configured and deployed for the dynamic and changing environment having broad spectrum of functionalities for the Verification of IFC models.**

Keywords- Conformance of IFC models; Building Code; MvdXML; BIM; Querying IFC models;

I. Introduction

Building codes are the rules and guidelines that specify the minimum acceptable level of safety, accessibility, general welfare, etc. of building models. Through building code and standards, organizations achieve their fundamental goal to protect public health, safety and general welfare as they relate to the construction and occupancy of buildings. The aim of validating Models is to align several specialized indexations of building components at both sides, assuming that they deal with the same abstract concepts or physical objects, but according to their separate representation prisms. Building Code is vital to detect non-compliance elements in the IFC model and to ensure its quality and reliability in the entire life-cycle of BIM [1], [2]. Since many years, *Industry Foundation Classes* (IFC) has been used by the *Architecture, Engineering and Construction* (AEC) industry for the building model representation. IFC is the complete and fully stable open and international standard for exchanging building data [3]. IFC has been designed to process a building's data model throughout its entire life cycle and to allow the inter-exchange of an information model without loss or distortion of data. Building SMART organization aims at publishing IFC and related buildingSMART data model standards. The buildingSMART data model standards are developed by the Model Support Group, and the implementation activities are coordinated by the Implementation Support Group [4]. Together, both groups organize the IFC software certification process. It aims to be a global standard for the BIM data exchanges.

To determine the quality of an IFC model after it has been developed and to fully automate quality assessment according to the French building code compliance regulations of IFC models is one of the goal of our enterprise, *Centre Scientifique et Technique du Bâtiment (CSTB)*, through its research and development efforts. Building code compliance is a difficult job because it needs to check all building work must comply with the building codes (i.e., fire safety, accessibility, etc.). For this, verification each small IFC object must be tested to ensure its accuracy and validity along with test of overall IFC objects together in the IFC model. To achieve these goals, our research adopts a traditional approach using MvdXML [5]. The subset of the IFC schema needed to satisfy one or many Exchange Requirements of the AEC industry is called *Model View Definition* (MVD). The XML format used to publish the concepts and associated rules is MvdXML and it is regarded as an open standard [5]. It can be used with the IfcDoc tool [18] developed by the buildingSMART International to read and write MvdXML and to provide a graphical user interface for defining all content within MvdXML. It is aimed to improve the consistent and computer-interpretable definition of MVD as true subsets of the IFC Specification with the enhanced definition of concepts. MVDs provide additional rules for the IFC validation and focus on extracting integral model subsets for IFC implementation purposes. The buildingSMART is willing to support construction domain developers in reusing its leading openBIM standard IFC as a baseline to set up specific data exchange protocols to satisfy exchange requirements in the industry. The buildingSMART International has developed IfcDoc tool for creating Model View Definitions. Based on the newly developed MvdXML standard, just Model View Definitions can now be easily developed using the IfcDoc tool. The tool and methodology can be applied to all IFC releases (IFC2x3, IFC4, etc.). For the validation of an IFC file against a particular model view, IfcDoc tool user interface displays a pane on the right side containing object instances within the file matching definitions selected in the tree view. The end-user can generate a report in the HTML format indicating if the file is valid according to the specified model view, and detailing what passes or fails. IfcDoc tool and conformance checking by MvdXML technology is a good candidate for the simple rules on small IFC models. Although it fulfills lots of requirements for the code compliance of IFC models but still there is a gap which needs to be fulfilled. We took this opportunity to fulfill this gap and propose certain extensions. Finally, in this paper, we suggest going beyond MvdXML and present a need of an approach based on Semantic Web technologies that can easily be extended, configured and deployed for the dynamic and changing environment having broad spectrum of functionalities for the Verification of IFC models.

The rest of paper is organized as follows. Section 2 presents related work. Section 3 discusses a usecase and extensions in the MvdXML for the conformance checking of IFC models. Section 4 points several limitations of MvdXML validation rules and discusses to go beyond MvdXML. Section 5 concludes this paper.

II. Related Work

Code Compliance checking is targeted by the industry and researchers in order to provide the facilities to stake-holders like the delivery of high quality IFC model to ensure more accurate, consistent and reliable results in the life-cycle of BIM. In the BIM based research literature, there are three ways for the conformance checking of IFC models as discussed by Pauwels and Zhang [16]. First, we have the '*hard coded rule checking*' where rules are integrated inside the application. This approach is adopted by Solibri Model Checker [17] and IfcDoc tool [18] along with the MvdXML rules. The second approach is '*rule checking by querying*' the IFC model followed by K.R. Bouzidi et al [19]. In this approach, BIM is interrogated by rules, which are formalized directly into SPARQL queries. The third is a semantic rule checking approach with dedicated rule languages (such as SWRL [7], Jess [24] or N3Logic [25]) adopted by H. Wicaksono et al. [20] based on SWRL rules, Pauwels et al. [21] based on N3Logic rules and M. Kadolsky et al. [22].

Besides these researches, recent years revealed some contributions based on Semantic Web technologies. SWOP-PMO project is one of recent contributions that use formal methodology based on the Semantic Web standards and technologies [14]. It uses OWL/RDF to represent the knowledge, and SPARQL [8] queries and Rule Interchange Format (RIF) to represent the rules. The RDF/OWL representation is not derived from the written knowledge but has to be remodeled in accordance with the rules of OWL/RDF. There are some other works for the semantic enrichment of ontologies in the construction and building domain. Emani et al. proposed an ontology-based framework for generating an OWL Description Logic (DL) [23] expression of a given concept from its natural language definition automatically [15]. Their framework also takes into account an IFC ontology and the resultant DL expression is built by using the existing IFC entities. To enable the compliance checking of the repository through the digital building model, Fahad et al. have contributed a framework for mapping certification rules over BIM [11]. They aimed to align several specialized indexations of building components at both sides, by extending IfcOWL ontology with bSDD vocabulary (i.e., synonyms and description) as enriched IfcOWL ontology to deal with the same abstract concepts or physical objects. Fahad et al. also investigated semantic web approach by using SWRL and traditional approach by the use of IfcDoc tool and analyzed that the semantic web technique represent more global scope with larger visibility of querying for the validation of IFC models [12].

III. Extensions in the MvdXML Checker

An MvdXML document contains an instance of mvd:MvdXML as a main element, which defines a set of reusable concept templates, mvd:ConceptTemplate, and a set of model view definitions, mvd:ModelView. Each model view defines an applicable schema like IFC2X3 or IFC4 and may set a link to a base view definition if it is an add-on view. The validation of IFC building models is vital in the BIM-based collaboration processes and can be done via IfcDoc tool. Using IfcDoc tool with the MvdXML rules, an end-user performs three steps of automatic control sequence. The IfcDoc engine loads an IFC file and MvdXML files containing rules, and then it executes defined rules over IFC model. Finally, it generates a report indicating compliance (compliant/non-compliant) of each item under the rule. It assigns each rule a green or red depending on whether the item is/is-not in compliance to the defined rules. Besides IfcDoc tool, an end-user can use standalone MvdXML Checker (a java-based research prototype) to meet the requirements of verification models. Working on different usecases, we found that we need extensions in the MvdXML Checker to meet the requirements of real world scenarios. The following subsections present motivation scenario and the extensions we made in the MvdXML checker.

A. *UseCase Scenario – conditions and constraints*

When we need to access the name/label of an IFCSpace, we can simply access the name attribute of the IFC schema. This is a very simple case which can be employed very easily. But there are some scenarios which we cannot implement with the current implementation of MvdXML. During the validation process we can have conditions and constraints in the rule for certain scenarios which is not supported by the MvdXML Checker. According to IAI, *"An IFCConstraint is used to define a constraint or limiting value or boundary condition that may be applied to an* *object or to the value of a property*". This element is defined within the elements mvd:EntityRule and mvd:AttributeRule and represents a restriction on an attribute, which may require the value, type, or collection size to have equality (or other comparison) to a literal value or referenced value. For example consider a scenario illustrated in Figure 1, where we can apply conditions and constraints on the IFCSpace. Figure 2 demonstrates the MvdXML of this small example. One can note that in MvdXML rule file, description="*" in the rule description demonstrates the presence of a condition and its absence represents the constraints. There can be very complex situation, for example, as depicted in Figure 3, a chain of hierarchy, where conditions and constraints are involved. Therefore, precise tackling of conditions and constraints should be analyzed and integrated properly in the MvdXML Checker.

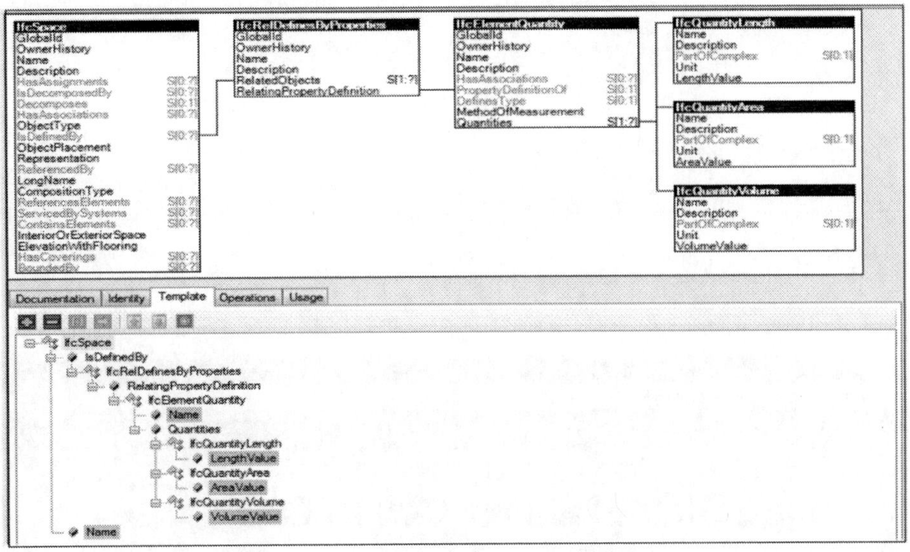

Figure 1. IFCSpace with various attributes

```
<ConceptTemplate uuid="f4a3a95e-fa59-41a7-83ad-5cff467b25bc" name="test" applicableSchema="IFC4" applicableEntity="IfcSpace">
  <Rules>
    <AttributeRule AttributeName="IsDefinedBy">
      <EntityRules>
        <EntityRule EntityName="IfcRelDefinesByProperties">
          <AttributeRules>
            <AttributeRule AttributeName="RelatingPropertyDefinition">
              <EntityRules>
                <EntityRule EntityName="IfcElementQuantity">
                  <AttributeRules>
                    <AttributeRule RuleID="name" Description="*" AttributeName="Name" />
                    <AttributeRule AttributeName="Quantities">
                      <EntityRules>
                        <EntityRule EntityName="IfcQuantityLength">
                          <AttributeRules>
                            <AttributeRule RuleID="length_value" Description="*" AttributeName="LengthValue" />
                          </AttributeRules>
                        </EntityRule>
                        <EntityRule EntityName="IfcQuantityArea">
                          <AttributeRules>
                            <AttributeRule RuleID="area_value" AttributeName="AreaValue" />
                          </AttributeRules>
                        </EntityRule>
                        <EntityRule EntityName="IfcQuantityVolume">
                          <AttributeRules>
                            <AttributeRule RuleID="volume_value" AttributeName="VolumeValue" />
                          </AttributeRules>
                        </EntityRule>
                      </EntityRules>
                    </AttributeRule>
                  </AttributeRules>
                </EntityRule>
              </EntityRules>
            </AttributeRule>
          </AttributeRules>
        </EntityRule>
      </EntityRules>
    </AttributeRule>
    <AttributeRule RuleID="name" Description="*" AttributeName="Name" />
  </Rules>
 </ConceptTemplate>
</SubTemplates>
</ConceptTemplate>
```

Figure 2. MvdXML showing conditions and contraints

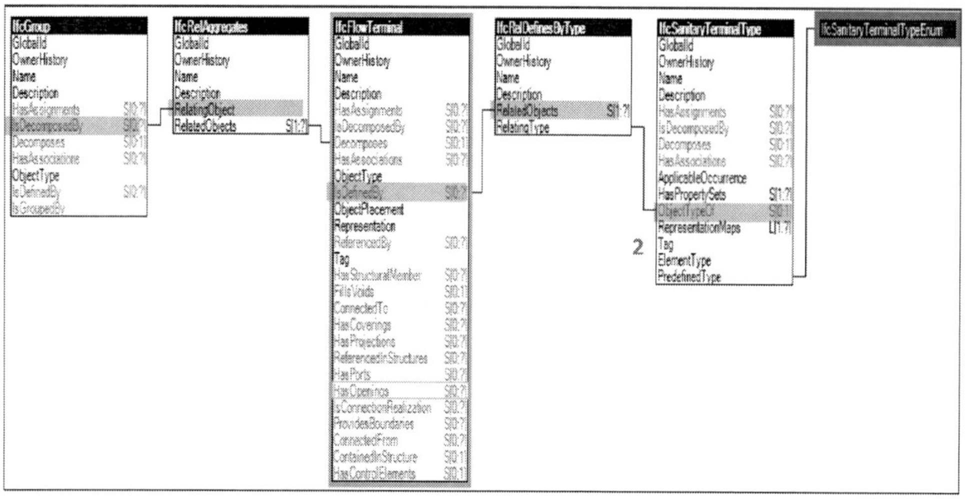

Figure 3. Applying conditions and constraints on the Attributes of an IFCSpace concept

Figure 4. Interface of output by the Extended MvdXML checker

B. *Extentioned MvdXML Checker as a WebService*

We have implemented several extensions including the use case defined above in the MvdXML checker and developed a web service [26] so that it can be used by end-users. First end-users upload an IFC model and choose to apply code compliance rules over their IFC model. Then, the checker executes control rules to verify chosen protocols on the input model by starting a web service. Web service executes the control rules and displays the results as an output in the html form as illustrated in Figure 4. Each of the rule that detects non-compliant elements are highlighted with the red color so that end-users would be alert in those particular cases. When one clicks on the red highlighted rule, the web service loads non-compliant elements with their *Guids, Names and Types*.

IV. NEED OF NEW IMPLEMENTATIONS FOR THE COMPLIANCE CHECKING OF IFC MODELS

This section highlights various limitations of MvdXML Checker and then discusses a real world use case scenario of verification rule which cannot be modeled by using MvdXML. Later in this section, we propose a semantic based solution for the building code conformance checking of IFC models.

A. *Limitations of MvdXML Checker*

Complex nature of IFC makes the information retrieval difficult and as a consequence it affects the validation process of MvdXML rules. Many tasks for an IFC model, such as information retrieval, model validation, etc., do not achieve real-time performance in the real-world BIM scenarios. There are many drawbacks of MvdXML for extracting building views such as: lack of logical formalisms, solely consideration of IFC schema and MVD-based view constructors are not very flexible and dynamic [6]. Verification by MvdXML rules are also very limited. Major limitations are identified such as restricted scope of applying conditions and constraints on several branches of an IFC model, poor geometric analysis of an IFC model, lack of mathematical calculations, support of only static verification of a model, etc. It does not show the cause or provide mechanisms for reasoning the inconsistencies or anomalies. However, on the other hand, Semantic Web technologies, especially SWRL or SPARQL, allow for the semantic verification of IFC models to enable the compliance checking of IFC construction models with fast querying performance. The next section will show motivation for the semantic based verification of IFC models.

B. *Need of New Semantic Implementations*

While working with the MvdXML and IFC tools, we realized that there is no support to build new concept and/or high level vocabulary dynamically or create a new rule using existing concepts. For example, a simple rule that is based on *'Highest Storey'* would neither be possible with IfcDoc tool nor with the MVDXML specification. But, if we process an IfcModel and build a semantic repository with the geometry information and materialize high level vocabulary via SPARQL Rules and Queries then we can build verification rules over the *Highest Storey*. With the help of Sparql rules on the geometry data (i.e., minimum and maximum values of X, Y and Z coordinates) of IFC objects, we can infer elements which are *Above or Below* with respect to each other. Once we can infer IFC objects then *"Not Exists {B above A}"* concludes A as a *Highest Storey* having nothing over it. Figure 5 illustrates this scenario.

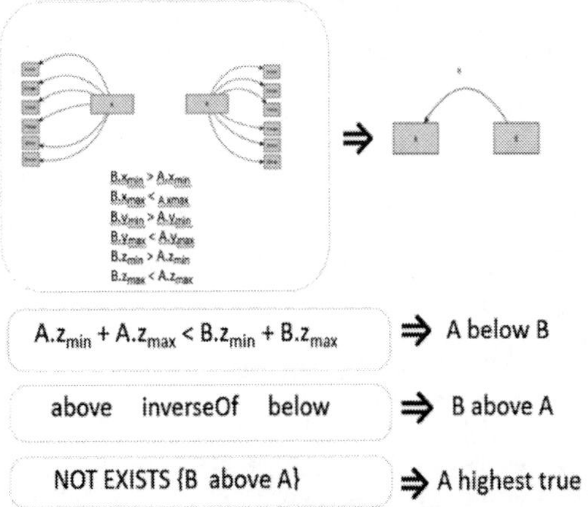

Figure 5. Semantic illustration of Highest Storey Concept using geometry data from an IFC model

Besides building verification rules over geometry data, querying semantic model is faster and gives a good run-time. One can customize queries easily and according to requirements. Using MvdXML, there is no intermediate state and IfcDoc tool gives no explanation for the reason of non-compliance. On the other hand, the Semantic Web technology is a good compromise between development efforts and opportunities. The graphical representation of RDF allows rules to be more intuitive and more efficient to reason and execute. As SWRL [7] and SPARQL [8] are W3C recommendations, a lot more functionalities are added to meet the requirements of the real world scenarios. For example, one can perform calculations in SWRL, which we cannot do in MvdXML. In addition, we can also define new attributes and elements, evolve the existing values, and give them values based on the initial axioms in the repository and store them back in our repository for further processing. In addition, many complex verification rules execute on the combination of IFC objects or depend on small rules, but this is not much flexible and most of the time concatenation of conditions and constraints is not possible in the IfcDoc using MVDXML specification.

C. *Work in Progress – Semantic based Verification*

To meet the requirement of semantic checking, we have implemented semantic based approach for the building code compliance. We have used IFC-to-RDF-Converter developed by Pauwels and Oraskari [13] to get a semantic repository (RDF triplets) [10] equivalent from an IFC model. We apply filtration to get an RDF equivalent compact triplet file to avoid several IFC elements, such as Person, Address, Material-List, etc. Then, we extract all geometry data from the input IFC model by using BIM-Server plugins [27]. BIM-Server is an open source toolkit to work with the IFC models and provides two plugins (i.e., *IFCOpenShell* and *IFC Engine DLL*) for the extraction of geometry data. Once we gather all triplets (i.e., Filtered RDF file of IFC model and Triplets of Geometry data), we load them into the Stardog triple store [9] for the fast querying, searching, and analyzing of RDF triplets. Over these triplets, we build our high level vocabulary by using SPARQL rules (e.g., highest storey concept explained above). Finally, we formalized verification rules into SPARQL queries which bring triplets (i.e., non-conformance elements) in the case of non-compliance of building code. The whole architecture is illustrated in Figure 6. We build several test cases comprise of different queries on different sizes of IFC models by the traditional approach via IfcDoc and the ontology-based semantic approach via SPARQL. From the initial results, we conclude that SPARQL queries are flexible for retrieving data and do the validation in an optimized way giving better run-time as compared to the traditional approach via IfcDoc. But the conversion from IFC to RDF and then storage of triples into stardog takes time. But, once the stardog triple store is loaded with the data, it is much faster querying and validation of IFC models. SPARQL queries can be modified easily with the new or customized conditions and constraints for the conformance checking against the triple store. Besides flexibility, reasoning is another advantage of Semantic Web technology, as the IfcDoc tool does not provide any justification. With queries and rules, we can identify reasons of inconsistencies and anomalies via RDF graph traversals.

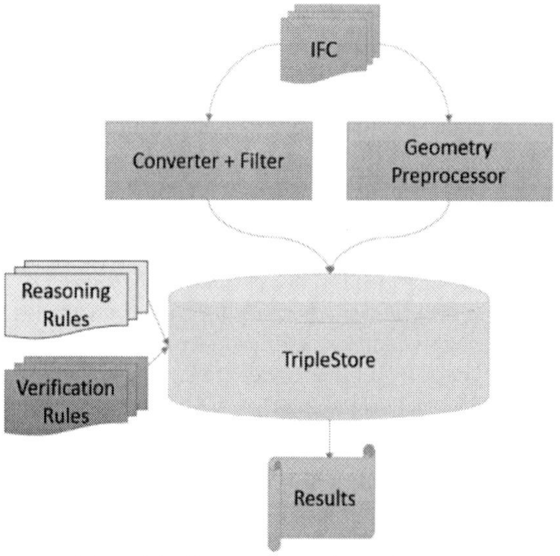

Figure 6. Architecture of semantic-based Approach

V. CONCLUSION AND FUTURE WORK

An IFC is a specific data format that aims at allowing the inter-exchange of an information model without loss or distortion of data. Building Code compliance is vital to ensure the quality and reliability of an IFC model. Building code compliance of IFC models is a hot issue for the researchers. One of the ways to apply code compliance of IFC files is by the use of MvdXML checker. However, current implementation needs further extensions so that all the rule specifications can be covered and tested. In this paper, we presented extensions we made in the implementation of MvdXML Checker available for the validation of IFC models. The proposed extensions were implemented in the form of a web service. End-users can invoke this service to check code-compliance according to their own rules over their desired IFC models. Finally, this paper also addresses the need of a semantic approach towards the automatic verification requirements to warn the non-conformities as a hot challenge. Our on-going research work is to develop and investigate a semantic web approach. We transform an IFC model into a RDF model and query on RDF triplets to meet the requirements of code compliance. It is obvious that only a well-engineered IFC model that passes code compliance can serve best in the entire life-cycle of BIM.

REFERENCES

[1] V. Rebekka, J. Stengel, and F. Schultmann, "Building Information Modeling (BIM) for existing buildings—Literature review and future needs," Automation in construction, vol. 38, pp. 109-127, 2014, doi: 10.1016/j.autcon.2013.10.023

[2] C. Eastman, P. Teicholz, R. Sacks, and K. Liston, "BIM Handbook: A Guide to Building Information Modeling for Owners, Managers, Designers, Engineers, and Contractors," Hoboken, New Jersey, Wiley, 2008.

[3] V. Thein, Industry Foundation Classes (IFC), "BIM Interoperability Through a Vendor-Independent File Format," A Bentley White Paper, September 2011.

[4] Building Smart, International home of openBIM, https://www.buildingsmart.org/standards/ [last access: june 2018]

[5] T. Chipman, T. Liebich, and M. Weise, "MvdXML specification of a standardized format to define and exchange MVD with exchange requirements and validation Rules," version 1.1 Final, Febrary 2016. Available at: http://www.buildingsmart-tech.org/downloads/mvdxml /mvdxml-1.1/final/mvdxml-1-1-documentation

[6] T. Mendes de Farias, A. Roxin, and C. Nicolle, "A Semantic Web Approach for defining Building Views," buildingSMART Summit Jeju, Korea, 28 Sept, 2016.

[7] I. Horrocks, P.F. Patel-Schneider, H. Boley, S. Tabet, B. Grosof, and M. Dean, "SWRL: A Semantic Web Rule Language Combining OWL and RuleML," 2004.

[8] SPARQL Query Language for RDF, http://www.w3.org/TR/rdf-sparql-query/, 2008. [last access: June 2018]

[9] Stardog, http://stardog.com/ [last access: June 2018]

[10] D. Brickley, R.V. Guha, and B. McBride, (2004). "RDF vocabulary description language 1.0: RDF Schema," W3C Recommendation 2004. [last access: June 2017]

[11] M. Fahad, Nicolas Bus., and F. Andrieux, "Towards Mapping Certification Rules over BIM," Proc. of the 33rd CIB W78 Conference, Brisbane, Australia, 2016.

[12] M. Fahad, N. Bus, F. Andrieux, "Towards Validation of IFC Models with IfcDoc and SWRL," In proc of The Twelfth International

Conference on Internet and Web Applications and Services (ICIW), italy. pp. 7-13, 2017.

[13] P. Pauwels and J. Oraskari, "IFC-to-RDF Converter" https://github.com/IDLabResearch/IFC-to-RDF-converter, [last access: June 2017]

[14] F. Josefiak, H. Bohms, P. Bonsma, and M. Bourdeau, "Semantic product modelling with SWOP's PMO, eWork and eBusiness in AEC," pp. 95-104

[15] C.K. Emani, C. Ferreira Da Silva, B. Fiès, P. Ghodous, and M. Bourdeau., "Automated Semantic Enrichment of Ontologies in the Construction Domain," Proc. of the 32nd CIB W78 Conference, Netherlands, 2015.

[16] P. Pauwels and S. Zhang, "Semantic Rule-Checking for regulation compliance checking: An overview of strategies and approaches," Proc. of the 32nd CIB W78 Conference, Netherlands, 2015.

[17] L. Khemlani, "Solibri model checker," AECbytes Product Review March 31, 2009

[18] IfcDoc Tool, available at: http://www.buildingsmart-tech.org/specifications/ specification-tools /IfcDoc-tool/IfcDoc-help-page-section/IfcDoc.pdf, 2012. [last access: June 2017]

[19] K. R., Bouzidi, B., Fies, C., Faron-Zucker, A. Zarli, and N. Le Thanh, "Semantic Web Approach to Ease Regulation Compliance Checking in Construction Industry," Future Internet, Special Issue Semantic Interoperability and Knowledge Building, 4 (3). pp. 830-851, 2012.

[20] H. Wicaksono, P., Dobreva, P. Häfner, and S. Rogalski, "Ontology development towards expressive and reasoning-enabled building information model for an intelligent energy management system," Proc. of the 5th KEOD, pp. 38-47. SciTePress, 2013.

[21] P. Pauwels, D. Van Deursen, R. Verstraeten, J. De Roo, R. De Meyer, R. Van de Walle, and J. Van Campenhout, "A semantic rule checking environment for building performance checking," Automation in Construction. 20 (5). pp. 506-518, 2011.

[22] M. Kadolsky, K. Baumgärtel, and R. J. Scherer, "An ontology framework for rule-based inspection of eeBIM-systems," Procedia Engineering. vol. 85, 2014, pp. 293-301, doi:10.1016/j.proeng.2014.10.554.

[23] OWL 2 Web Ontology Language Document Overview (Second Edition), W3C Recommendation 11 December 2012, https://www.w3.org/TR/owl2-overview/ [last access: June 2018]

[24] E. Friedman-Hill, "Jess in Action: Rule Based Systems in Java," Manning Publications. ISBN 1-930110-89-8, 2003

[25] T. Berners-Lee, D. Connolly, L. Kagal, Y. Scharf, and J. Hendler, "N3Logic: A logical framework for the World Wide Web," Theory and Practice of Logic Programming. vol. 8 (3), 2008, pp. 249-269, doi:10.1017/S1471068407003213.

[26] Extended MvdXML Checker as as web service: https://svc-bim-checker.dev.coplus.fr/CheckerService/v2/ui

[27] Open source BIMserver-plugin available at: https://github.com/opensourceBIM/IfcOpenShell- BIMserver-plugin [last access: June 2018]

Improving Default Risk Information System with TensorFlow

Cláudio Augusto Silveira Lélis
Scientific Initiation Program
IMES / Faculty ImesMercosur
Juiz de Fora, Brazil
e-mail: claudioaugustolelis@imes.org.br

André Luiz Silveira Lopardi
Master's Program in Business Administration
FUMEC University
Belo Horizonte, Brazil
e-mail: andrelopardi@yahoo.com.br

***Abstract*—The decision process is essential in the granting of credit. The right decision can be critical in reducing financial losses. DeRis (Default Risk Information System) is an information system designed to support activities in the management of default risk. The main component is a predictive model of default based on indicators. Currently, the system has been improved allowing models of the TensorFlow tool. Based on real datasets, the default model and the predictive models of the TensorFlow tool was evaluated for different types of indicators. The results show that a model optimization was possible through the adjustment of the hyperparameters offered by TensorFlow, with 240 distinct combinations being tested between these hyperparameters. Although the results are associated with the data and the design of the experiment conducted, they were considered positive and promising for future work.**

Keywords*–*Indicators; Financial Management; Knowledge-based Decision-making; Default Prediction Model; TensorFlow.

I. INTRODUCTION

Over time, companies have been adapting to changes while remaining competitive and profitable in an increasingly crowded market. Applying constant investments in the area of Information Technology, financial institutions seek to offer products to their customers in a fast, safe and high technological value. Always attentive to high performance and information security, especially with the large volume of data. On the other hand, customers can count on the trust, performance and safety expected of a financial institution [1].

In this period, while efficiency has gained prominence, companies continue to analyze risks, reduce losses, and maximize efficiency. For instance, a financial institution should identify risks in lending situations, draw conclusions as to the borrower's ability to repay, and make recommendations regarding the best structuring and type of loan to be granted in the light of the applicant's financial needs [2]. In a scenario of uncertainties and incomplete information, risk analysis involves the ability to establish a decision rule to guide the granting of credit.

According to [3], credit risk is associated with the risk of a borrower or counterpart being defaulted. Thus, in the position of financial intermediaries, banks must act in a way that minimizes risk and enables fairer terms of credit acquisition. The difficulty of performing guarantees and recovering credit has led to uncertainty and instability in the market, making default the biggest cost of a bank's financial margin.

Although there are different concepts, default in the context of this research can be understood as a delay of more than 90 days in the liabilities assumed with a financial institution [4].

The use of default prediction models serves to measure, monitor and predict the financial situation of companies, reducing uncertainties and doubts in decision making [5]. The models are constructed with the support of statistical techniques and applied to analyze their dependent variables.

For the survival of financial institutions, the correct decision to grant credit is essential [6]. It is important to anticipate and reduce default [7], since the losses from unsuccessful credits should be covered by charging high interest rates on new concessions. Therefore, using a default risk forecasting model for a financial institution and linking management strategies to the reality of the borrower can be critical in assessing credit risk and reducing financial losses.

An information system, called DeRis [8], was developed aimed to support activities in the management of default risk. It encompasses a default prediction model based on conflict indicators, management, and financial indicators, a reasoner and visualization elements. Through the storage of decisions, a knowledge database is maintained. Thus, a significant amount of data must be collected, processed and stored over time, for proper monitoring of the indicators involved. DeRis offers this information through interactive visualizations, assisting the process of discovering knowledge through these data, aiming decision making.

Since its inception, the DeRis system has been validated, tested and applied to actual data, provided by a bank. This experience is reported in Lelis and Lopardi [8]. The bank that offered its data and became a partner of this research, will be called Zak bank for confidentiality issues.

Zak Bank focuses its activities on resource generation and credit analysis. It also seeks to meet the consumption and investment needs of individuals and companies. Considering the impact and risk of a customer becoming defaulted, it has become important for Zak Bank to monitor companies in the economic environment and manage a possible default.

There was a concern that the prediction model, used in DeRis system, specializes in the data provided by ZAK bank. As a consequence, the system could become static and fitted only to the reality of this context. To avoid this situation, the need to incorporate new model options into the system has increased. Moreover, it would also be necessary to submit the system to different datasets associated with different indicators.

In this scenario, the incorporation of the TensorFlow tool [9] could be a good opportunity for improvement for the DeRis system. It is an open source software library for high-performance digital computing. Its flexible architecture enables the easy deployment of computing across multiple processing unit platforms and desktops to server clusters, for mobile devices and peripherals. It comes with strong support for machine learning and deep learning, and the flexible numerical computing core is used in many other scientific domains. Given this, TensorFlow can offer more dynamism and speed to the DeRis system from its implementation in Python.

This article presents the improvements in DeRis system allowing models of the TensorFlow tool, and is structured by this introduction and Section 2 shows the background in which the proposal is inserted and some related work. Section 3 focuses on the improved components of the DeRis system. In Section 4, the carried out experiment is presented and Section 5 includes the final considerations.

II. Background

Through a survey of the specialized technical literature, it was possible to perceive that the researchers' interest in default risk models dates back to the 1930s [10][11]. Over the years, the pioneering work of Beaver [12] and especially Altman [13], boosted research in the 1970s with accounting indicators [14]–[18].

Changes in the world financial scenario since the 1990s, such as deregulation of interest rates and exchange rates, increased liquidity and increased competitiveness, especially in the banking sector, have increased the concern of financial institutions with the risk of default. Issues such as the emergence of new modeling techniques, the growing importance of credit risk management and the prevailing economic conditions, again aroused the interest in the area [19]–[22].

There are several techniques applied to credit risk forecasting models. They can be classified as discriminant analysis used in the model proposed by [13], neural networks as used by Lemos et al. [23] and replicated in the present paper.

Considering that a neural network has been replicated, it is necessary to present some basic concepts. Neural networks try to build internal representations of models or patterns detected in the data, which are generally not visible to the user. Neural Networks use a set of processing elements (nodes) analogous to neurons. These processing elements are interconnected in a network that can identify patterns in the data, that is, the network learns through experience, such as people. Existing Neural Networks models present one or more layers of neurons between the input and output layers, called hidden layers [24]. In these networks, each layer has a specific function. The output layer receives the results from the hidden layer and generates the final response. The network is formed by connecting the output of the neurons from the hidden layer to the input of the neurons of the output layer. The resulting structure is a weighted and directed graph. The weights as well as the functions that compute the internal state of a neuron (activation) can be modified by a process, called learning. This process is governed by a learning rule.

There are other techniques like multiple linear regression, linear programming, genetic algorithms, decision tree, logistic regression applied on the core model of DeRis system and, more recently, the analysis of survival.

Bonfim [25], for example, examined the determinants of corporate defaults in the banking sector in Portugal through the Logit or Probite Models of Survival Analysis. The study found that default is affected by specific characteristics of companies such as: capital structure, company size, profitability and liquidity, recent sales performance and investment policy. However, there was a significant improvement in the quality of the models, with the introduction of variables, especially the growth rate of all the riches produced in the country, the growth of lending, the average lending rate and the variation of stock market prices.

Bellovary et al. [26] investigated the main financial indicators used in studies to predict default and found the current liquidity present in 51 studies among those analyzed.

Years later, Jacobson et al. [27] presented a model based on macroeconomic factors. The nominal interest rate and the output gap are the two most important macroeconomic factors that affect corporate default. The authors also used the Earnings Before Interest, Taxes, Depreciation and Amortization (EBITDA) per Total Assets ratio, the interest coverage ratio, the leverage ratio, the total liability ratio and revenues, the ratio net assets and total liabilities and, finally, inventory turnover, as financial variables specific to each company.

Recently, Cunha et al. [28] carried out a national and an international survey where they investigate which features are required to enhance a credit scoring model in the context of a Brazilian retail enterprise, in order to find attributes that can improve the performance of classifier algorithms for credit granting. They conclude that additional financial and behavioral data increase defaulting prediction performance on credit granting.

From the identified models, as well as the concepts of credit and risk, it should be noted that the default forecast models, mostly, have financial indicators as explanatory variables. Therefore, creating a model without taking such indicators into account would put its effectiveness in question.

III. DeRis System

The proposed DeRis system arose from the need to predict the financial situation of companies to avoid default, as well as support managers and financial institutions in making decisions regarding the granting of credit.

The details of the system, as well as the features and data flow between each of the components were detailed in [8]. For this reason, only an overview will be presented. Then we will focus on improvements made with TensorFlow.

Figure 1 shows an overview of the DeRis system architecture, after the improvement process with its main components.

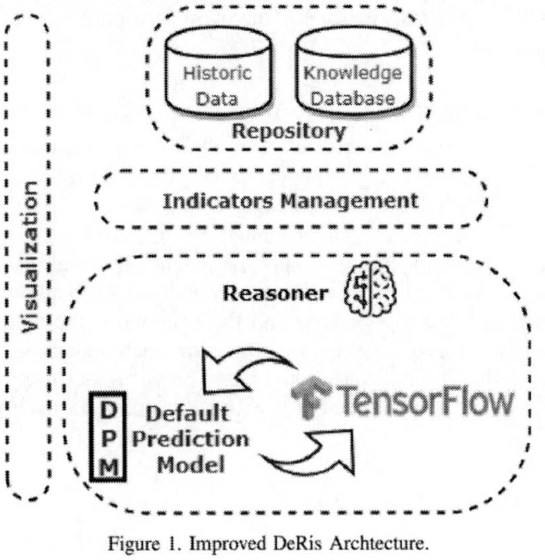

Figure 1. Improved DeRis Archtecture.

The information flow, while using the system, starts in

the repository that stores the historical data of the indicators. Additional information, such as a brief description and the indicator classification are also stored. Indicator management is performed to determine which indicators will be used in the selected prediction model. This choice is made considering the possibility of calculating the indicator with the available data.

The machine learning module is triggered and the selection of the default forecast model is enabled by the system. Reasoner gives managers the gain of information between raw data and model results. Moreover, Reasoner helps managers interpret the information generated during the process. Finally, the visualizations show the results and analyzes made by Reasoner and, through interaction elements, managers can associate control measures with the indicators.

The decisions taken during the process of using the system, as well as the information generated, are stored in a knowledge database, in order to feed the system and support future decisions.

The DeRis system presented a single model, at its core, based on Logistic Regression. In the construction and training phase of the model, the insertion or removal of some indicator can generate different results. Even the logistic regression model may present changes in the result. A new feature added to the system allows the storage of the decision, the indicators with their values, as well as the generated model. This measure aims to adjust the choice of indicators with the models provided by the TensorFlow tool, achieving better results.

A. Indicators Management

This is an important component of the system. It identifies the indicators whose data is stored, its additional information and mainly the classification that assists the Reasoner in the analyzes. Through these data, a feature of this component is to relate the indicator to the way of collecting, or calculating, its value.

All stored indicators are candidates to participate in the model. It is necessary to make the selection of the indicators when starting the monitoring of a company, or through previous decisions, the own component is capable of selects the indicators.

B. Visualization

The views offered by the DeRis system can now be triggered from any component of the system, and support attributes that can be measured in real time.

Through interaction elements, it is possible to select a point in the line graph and obtain contextual information, such as: the future trend of the default probability, the values of each indicator, the model used and the decision taken at the time, if any. Moreover, the percentage of each indicator, colored according to the variation to the previous occurrence. This feature allows the analysis of the variability in the influence of indicators.

C. Machine Learning Module

The components responsible for intelligence, knowledge discovery and information interpretation have been aggregated and now integrate the Machine Learning Module along with the TensorFlow tool.

1) Reasoner Phase: Assuming that there are indicators A, B and C. However, only the data for indicators A and C are available. Given this, *would it be possible to replace B? Which indicator could replace it?* Questions like these that Reasoner tries to answer with their analysis.

These questions can be answered by the Reasoner due to information such as: the class to which the indicator belongs, the unit of indicator measure, its degree of influence on the default and decisions taken previously after the exchange of indicators.

Another important function is to relate a moment of the past with a description of the decision made and what were the critical indicators for default, based on historical data and the knowledge base.

Although the review process is transparent to the user, the decision to replace an indicator is performed by the manager, when necessary, whenever a company's monitoring begins.

With the new version of the system, Reasoner has acquired a new feature. Before the data is stored in the knowledge base, it is responsible for mapping between the attributes with their values and the chosen model with its execution parameters.

2) Default Prediction Model: This is the legacy core model based on conflict, management and financial indicators, classified in the indicators management stage.

The technique applied by the model is logistic regression [29] that allows analyzing the effect of one or more independent variables on a dichotomous dependent variable, representing the presence or absence of a characteristic. In this way, it describes the relationship between several independent variables. According to this theory, the model calculates the probability of default, given by (1):

$$ProbDefault(yes) = \frac{e^{\eta}}{1 + e^{\eta}} \tag{1}$$

Where η depends on the indicators and data available for the logistic regression calculation.

3) TensorFlow: TensorFlow is a tool for machine learning with vast majority built in Python. It contains a wide range of functionality and provides many APIs. An important one is the Estimator API which provide scalable, high-performance models. Working as an interface for creating and executing machine learning algorithms.

Considering that TensorFlow is designed primarily for deep neural network models, it is necessary to analyze the hyperparameters that can be used in the training process to tune the model.

During training, the train method usually processes the examples several times. In addition, training works best if the training examples are in random order. Therefore, it is good practice to ensure that the data will be well scrambled.

The train method processes a batch of examples at a time and sets the default batch size to 100, which means that the batch method will concatenate groups of 100 samples. The ideal lot size depends on the problem. As a general rule, smaller batch sizes often allow the method to train the model more quickly at (or sometimes even) expense of accuracy.

The steps argument tells train to stop training after the specified number of iterations. Increasing steps increases the amount of time the model will train. Counter-intuitively, training a model longer does not guarantee a better model. The number of steps to train is a hyperparameter that can be tuned. Choosing the right number of steps usually requires both experience and experimentation.

In the next section, there will be shown the evaluation in which these parameters could be tested in different configurations.

IV. Evaluation

This Section presents the experimental study conducted. According to the Goal/Question/Metric approach (GQM) [30] the goal can be stated as: **Analyze** the DeRis system **in order to** verify the feasibility of using the improvements made **with respect to** the implementation of the TensorFlow tool offering option to the default forecast model **from the point of view of** managers and professionals of financial institutions **in the context of** credit analysis and default risk.

In this sense, the metrics defined to verify the fit quality of the models were the mean error and mean accuracy, like used by [23].

The experiment was proposed based on a set of real data collected from documentary sources by [23]. The Dataset was chosen because it presents attributes different from those previously studied in the DeRis system. In addition, because it is available for access and have the application parameters and methodology explained in order to facilitate the replication attempt.

Therefore, in this work, the historical data of 339 corporate clients were used, including micro, small and medium-sized enterprises, of which 73 are defaulters and 266 debt free companies. From each of them, 24 information (between cadastral and company accounting) were extracted, which will be specified below.

- **Restrictions on behalf of the company:** Represents the existence of restrictions and can be categorized between YES or NO.
- **Restrictions lowered in the last five years on behalf of the company:** Represents the existence of lowered restrictions and can be categorized between YES or NO.
- **Time of account:** Defined as a numeric value in Months.
- **Sector of activity:** Defined as a category between between Trade (1), Industry (2) or Services (3).
- **Uptime:** Categorized in sets of years where: More than 9 years (1), From 6 to 9 years (2), From 3 to 5 years (3), From 1 to 2 years (4) and Less than 1 year (5).
- **Number of employees:** Defined as a numeric value.
- **Company headquarters (property):** Categorized between Own (1), Rented (2) or Provided (3)
- **Neighborhood:** Categorized between Downtown (1) or Other (2).
- **Main customers:** Categorized between Individuals (1), Companies (2) or Mixed (3).
- **Annual gross sales:** represented by a numeric value.
- **Customer in another bank:** Indicates if the company is also customer in another borrower and can be categorized between YES or NO.
- **Real estate:** Defined as a numeric value.
- **Movable property:** Defined as a numerical value.
- **Business insurance:** can be categorized between YES or NO.
- **Financial applications:** can be categorized as Greater than 8,000 (1), From 8,000 to 4,000 (2), From 4,000 to 2,000 (3), Less than 2,000 (4) and no applications (5)
- **Term sales:** can be categorized as Less than 20% (1) or More than 20% (2).
- **Credit experience:** can be categorized as Greater than 2 years (1), Less than 2 years (2) or No experience (3)
- **Account history:** can be categorized as Normal (1), Checks returned (2), New customer (3), Small frequent delays (4)
- **Company members have restrictions:** it can be categorized between YES or NO.
- **Members of the company had restrictions lowered in the last five years:** it can be categorized between YES or NO.
- **Partnership between spouses:** It indicates the existence of society and can be categorized between YES or NO.
- **Real estate on behalf of partners:** Defined as a numerical value.
- **Movable property on behalf of the partners:** Defined as a numerical value.
- **Assigned risk:** a concept defined by the borrower, which stipulates the minimum guarantees required in credit operations. Categorized into levels by a scale where, 1 is the best and 5 is the worst concept.

A. Analysis

In this section, we present the replication made from the data and the methodology adopted. As well as an optimization in relation to the parameters that allow to tune the model. And, finally, a test with a balanced data set. A comparison between them with regard to their performances in obtaining the results are discussed and presented at the end.

1) Replication: Eight sets of tests were performed in total. The first test included information from all 339 companies. In the others, the data were separated into two sets: a training with data from 306 companies, composed of 241 non-defaulting companies and 65 defaulters, and another set for testing with information from 33 companies, composed of 25 non-defaulting companies and 8 defaulters. Except in the first case, in each of the tests performed, the sets were randomly generated in order to avoid any kind of induction of results. The difference between each test was the number of times the samples were shuffled. For the first test were shuffled once to the second they were shuffled twice each set of data and so on until the eighth test.

The training was carried out through a network of multiple layers, varying the following parameters:

- **Number of iterations (steps):** in each set of tests, the Neural Network was trained with 100, 1,000, 2,000, 4,000, 6,000, 8,000 and 10,000 iterations;
- **Number of intermediate neurons in the network:** in each test performed, the Neural Network was trained first without the intermediate layer and then using 2, 4, 6, 8 and 10 neurons in the intermediate layer. For

each test performed, a random set of initial weights was used;
- **Learning rate:** constant equal to 0.01;
- **Momentum rate:** It was decided not to use it.

Considering in this replication the random characteristic in the selection of the datasets this indicates that it is not possible to say if the same samples are in the same sets used by Lemos et al. [23]. For this reason, the results found in each set of tests were aggregated by the mean of the accuracy and are depicted in Table I.

TABLE I. REPLICATION RESULTS

Mean accuracy of	Lemos et al. [23]	Replication
Train set	95.91%	96.58%
Test set	90.04%	83.12%

The analysis shows an accuracy gain of 0.67 in the replicate model training set. In relation to the test set, the replicated model presented a difference in the accuracy of 6.92 of the results presented by Lemos et al. [23]. After such observations, it was necessary to analyze if there is statistical relevance in the variations found by the means and, furthermore, a hypothesis test was conducted.

Initially, the Shapiro-Wilk normality test was performed on the results obtained by Lemos et al. [23] and then, on the replication results. Considering that the data had no normal distribution, a non-parametric test was applied. The Mann-Whitney test, at a significance level of 5%, obtained a p-value of 0.533. Thus, the null hypothesis was accepted that there are no statistically significant differences for the samples. Therefore, the means are statistically equivalent.

2) Optimization: In order to verify the influence of the hyperparameters in the model, an optimization was proposed from the same sets generated for the replication and the same shuffle strategy. The training was carried out varying the following parameters:

- **Number of iterations (steps):** in each set of tests, the Neural Network was trained up to 15,000 iterations;
- **Number of hidden layers:** in each test performed, the Neural Network was trained first without a hidden layer and then using 1, 2 and 3 hidden layers, with the same number of neurons;
- **Number of intermediate neurons in the network:** the same as used for Replication;
- **Learning rate:** the same as used for Replication;
- **Momentum rate:** the same as used for Replication.

The results found in each set of tests were aggregated by the mean of the accuracy and are shown in Table II.

TABLE II. OPTIMIZATION RESULTS

Mean accuracy of	Replication	Optimization
Train set	96.58%	99.71%
Test set	83.12%	85.71%

3) Balanced: It is worth noting that there was a concern about the validity of the results found due to the fact that the sample was unbalanced, with 73 companies in default and 266 companies free of debt.

Therefore, it was decided to repeat the process with a new sample that was balanced and thus obtain a revalidation of the model. For the construction of this sample, all the defaulters were selected (73) and a random sample was made in the 266 so that 73 were selected. In order to guarantee the external and internal validity of the results found, a 8-steps of shuffle was used.

The results found in each set of tests were aggregated by the mean of the accuracy, compared with Replication and Optimization results and they are shown in Table III.

TABLE III. BALANCED SAMPLE RESULTS

Mean accuracy of	Replication	Optimization	Balanced
Train set	96.58%	99.71%	99.27%
Test set	83.12%	85.71%	87.50%

B. Lessons Learned

Considering the improvement process applied to the DeRis system, the process of preparing the indicators and the implementation of the evaluations, some lessons learned should be highlighted.

Although evaluating the visualizations was not the goal of the experiment, it is worth noting that they fit the new indicators and data with success.

Data Interoperability: The DeRis system was originally implemented in Java. However, the operation of TensorFlow, based on Python language, was transparent to the end user.

During the evaluation process, the possibility of setting up and managing indicators of different types from those shown in [8] was verified through the Indicator Manager.

The manipulation and representation of the data was facilitated. Avoid changing the data type to do the representation. Just load the data into the model.

Optimizing models is possible through configuration variables. Such optimization reduces the error in accuracy. However, the task of finding a good setup is not trivial. It is worth remembering that during the evaluation, between the replication and optimization phase, 240 combinations were tested, from the variation of 4 parameters.

Although the goal is not to replace the decision maker, the improvement process conducted in the DeRis system is an important tool in the management of the generated knowledge. The decisions taken generate information that re-feed the entire system. At the same time it adds value by allowing different perceptions of the data through each model.

V. CONCLUSION AND FUTURE WORK

The task of granting or not credit is and will always be difficult. Data Mining Techniques such as Neural Networks have proved to be very valuable tools for bank credit analysts. They become essential, combined with systems like DeRis and credit analyst experience.

An experimental study was conducted. The evaluation process was divided into three stages. Initially, the replication of the test applied by Lemos et al. [23] was successfully performed. In the following steps, only the results obtained by TensorFlow, through the DeRis system, were used for the comparison. Thus, the second step was to find the best values for the hyperparameters and obtain an optimized model with more accurate results. In the third step, the construction of a model trained from a balanced data set took place.

A threat to validity of the study is associated to the universe of variables previously defined and the particularities of the data under study. Even with a sign that is totally favorable to the granting of credit to a new customer, it may become a defaulting customer. Other factors, such as an accident (fire, theft or other) can interfere with the company's behavior in relation to commitments. An example like this is difficult to predict considering the analyzed data.

Although the implementation of the neural network was in a programming language different from that adopted by Lemos et al. [23], some precautions were taken to reduce the possibility of variation in the results obtained by replication and, as a consequence, reduce the effect of this possible threat to validity. Precautions such as the use of the same total data set, the same (random) selection strategy for the training set and the test set, as well as the same values of the network configuration parameters, considering the replication phase.

The results showed that the optimization was achieved with the adjustment of the hyperparameters offered by TensorFlow, with 240 different combinations being tested between these hyperparameters. Moreover, the model trained from a balanced set between classes obtained a better result even with a smaller number of instances. This provides opportunities for future research, for example, slicing the dataset to avoid models being trained with less representative instances. Although the results are associated with the data and the design of the experiment conducted, they were considered positive and promising. Therefore, the feasibility to apply TensorFlow in the context of DeRis was verified and, furthermore, it was possible to show that DeRis was prepared to deal with distinct indicators from those studied in [8].

As a contribution of this work, it was presented an application of TensorFlow tool in DeRis system that offers financial institutions an approach to encourage the use of different types of data and indicators, in the search for continuous improvement. Considering the experiment process, the replication carried out, in the first stage of the evaluation, can be considered a contribution of the present study since it increases the external validity of the tests conducted by Lemos et al. [23].

As future work we intend to use the system in a larger set of data to analyze its efficiency in the context of Big Data. In addition, expand the application of the system to other types of financial problems such as business bankruptcy, profit forecasting and value to be granted on credit.

REFERENCES

[1] C. G. Bernardo, "Loan system in brazilian financial institution-a soa application," in Information Technology: New Generations (ITNG), 2012 Ninth International Conference on. IEEE, 2012, pp. 293–298.

[2] D. Duffie and K. J. Singleton, Credit risk: pricing, measurement, and management. Princeton University Press, 2012.

[3] S. Westgaard and N. Van der Wijst, "Default probabilities in a corporate bank portfolio: A logistic model approach," European journal of operational research, vol. 135, no. 2, 2001, pp. 338–349.

[4] J. Bessis, Risk management in banking. John Wiley & Sons, 2011.

[5] M. T. Dugan and C. V. Zavgren, "How a bankruptcy model could be incorporated as an analytic," The CPA Journal, vol. 59, no. 5, 1989, p. 64.

[6] L. J. Gitman, R. Juchau, and J. Flanagan, Principles of managerial finance. Pearson Higher Education AU, 2015.

[7] M. Steiner, C. Carnieri, B. Kopittke, and P. S. Neto, "Probabilistic expert systems and neural networks in bank credit analysis," International Journal Of Operations And Quantitative Management, vol. 6, no. 4, 2000, pp. 235–250.

[8] C. A. S. Lélis and A. L. S. Lopardi, "Deris: Information system supporting the prediction of default risk in companies," in Information Technology-New Generations. Springer, 2018, pp. 325–332.

[9] M. Abadi et al., "Tensorflow: A system for large-scale machine learning." in OSDI, vol. 16, 2016, pp. 265–283.

[10] P. J. FitzPatrick, "A comparison of the ratios of successful industrial enterprises with those of failed companies," Certified Public Accountant, vol. 12, 1932, pp. 598–605.

[11] R. Smith and A. Winakor, Changes in the financial structure of unsuccessful industrial corporations. University of Illinois: Bureau of Business Research, 1935.

[12] W. H. Beaver, "Financial ratios as predictors of failure," Journal of accounting research, 1966, pp. 71–111.

[13] E. I. Altman, "Financial ratios, discriminant analysis and the prediction of corporate bankruptcy," The journal of finance, vol. 23, no. 4, 1968, pp. 589–609.

[14] R. O. Edmister, "An empirical test of financial ratio analysis for small business failure prediction," Journal of Financial and Quantitative analysis, vol. 7, no. 2, 1972, pp. 1477–1493.

[15] E. B. Deakin, "A discriminant analysis of predictors of business failure," Journal of accounting research, 1972, pp. 167–179.

[16] M. Blum, "Failing company discriminant analysis," Journal of accounting research, 1974, pp. 1–25.

[17] R. A. Eisenbeis, "Pitfalls in the application of discriminant analysis in business, finance, and economics," The Journal of Finance, vol. 32, no. 3, 1977, pp. 875–900.

[18] R. C. Moyer, "Forecasting financial failure: a re-examination," Financial Management, vol. 6, no. 1, 1977, p. 11.

[19] E. I. Altman, G. Marco, and F. Varetto, "Corporate distress diagnosis: Comparisons using linear discriminant analysis and neural networks (the italian experience)," Journal of banking & finance, vol. 18, no. 3, 1994, pp. 505–529.

[20] P. Brockett, W. Cooper, L. Golden, and X. Xia, "A case study in applying neural networks to predicting insolvency for property and casualty insurers," Journal of the Operational Research Society, 1997, pp. 1153–1162.

[21] C. Y. Shirata, "Financial ratios as predictors of bankruptcy in japan: an empirical research," Tsukuba College of Technology Japan, vol. 1, no. 1, 1998, pp. 1–17.

[22] C. Lennox, "Identifying failing companies: a re-evaluation of the logit, probit and da approaches," Journal of economics and Business, vol. 51, no. 4, 1999, pp. 347–364.

[23] E. Prezepiorski Lemos, M. T. Arns Steiner, and J. C. Nievola, "Análise de crédito bancário por meio de redes neurais e árvores de decisão: uma aplicação simples de data mining. alternative title: Analysis of bank credit through neural networks and decision trees: a simple application of data mining," RAUSP, vol. 40, no. 3, 2005, pp. 225–234.

[24] J. A. Anderson, An introduction to neural networks. MIT press, 1995.

[25] D. Bonfim, "Credit risk drivers: Evaluating the contribution of firm level information and of macroeconomic dynamics," Journal of Banking & Finance, vol. 33, no. 2, 2009, pp. 281–299.

[26] J. L. Bellovary, D. E. Giacomino, and M. D. Akers, "A review of bankruptcy prediction studies: 1930 to present," Journal of Financial education, 2007, pp. 1–42.

[27] T. Jacobson, J. Lindé, and K. Roszbach, "Firm default and aggregate fluctuations," Journal of the European Economic Association, vol. 11, no. 4, 2013, pp. 945–972.

[28] S. C. Cunha, E. M. Carneiro, L. F. S. Mialaret, L. A. V. Dias, and A. M. da Cunha, "Investigating attribute assessment for credit granting on a brazilian retail enterprise," in Information Technology-New Generations. Springer, 2018, pp. 301–309.

[29] D. W. Hosmer Jr, S. Lemeshow, and R. X. Sturdivant, Applied logistic regression. John Wiley & Sons, 2014, vol. 398.

[30] V. R. Basili and D. M. Weiss, "A methodology for collecting valid software engineering data," IEEE Transactions on Software Engineering, vol. SE-10, no. 6, 1984, pp. 728–738.

The Potential of Blockchain for Transforming the Urgent and Emergency Care

Daniela America da Silva, Samara Cardoso dos Santos, Wilson Cristoni Neto, Luiz Coura, Robison Egydio Lopes Junior, Gildarcio Sousa Gonçalves, Jose Crisóstomo Ozório Junior, Leonardo Guimarães, Alyson Basilio, Fabio Kfouri, Breslei Max Reis da Fonseca, Juliana F. Pasquini Martinez, Anderson Gomes, Paulo Diego Barbosa da Silva, Johnny Marques, Luiz Alberto Vieira Dias, Adilson Marques da Cunha, Paulo Marcelo Tasinaffo

Electronic Engineering and Computing Department
Brazilian Aeronautics Institute of Technology
São José dos Campos, São Paulo, Brazil
Email: stagiho-bd@googlegroups.com

Abstract—**During the 1st Semester of 2018, at the Brazilian Aeronautics Institute of Technology (Instituto Tecnológico de Aeronáutica - ITA), a successful Collaborative Interdisciplinary Problem-Based Learning (Co-IPBL) experience took place. At that time, more than 20 undergrad and graduate students from 3 different courses within just 16 academic weeks had the opportunity of conceptualizing, modeling, developing, and testing a Computer System based upon Big Data, Blockchain Hyperledger, Micro-services, and other emerging technologies for government and private organizations. This Co-IPBL was performed with the participation of a medical technical team from the Hospital of Clinics at the Faculty of Medicine of the University of São Paulo focusing in Urgency and Emergency Care. The purpose of this system was to aggregate data from actors, such as External Regulations of Heath Care, Hospital Internal Regulation, Hospital Emergency, Urgency Care, and Urgency Institutes, by integrating them into just one decision making process, to improve Urgency and Emergency Care. This academic research project was named in Portuguese *Soluções Tecnológicas Aplicáveis ao Gerenciamento de Informações Hospitalares Ostensivas com Big Data - STAGIHO-DB*, meaning in English "Technological Solutions Applicable for Managing Ostensive Hospital Information with Big Data - TSA4MOHIBD. Differently from other existing university systems, Research Centers, Governmental Agencies, Public or Private systems, this one was academically developed and tested in just 16 calendar weeks, applying Scrum Agile Method and Value Engineering. This research work was stored in a Google site and implemented as a Proof of Concept (PoC), by using emerging technologies, such as the Blockchain Hyperledger, a common database of health care information that doctors and providers could access. It represents one example of how to address the old problem of teaching, learning, designing, and implementing complex intelligent systems to solve health care problems, by collaboratively working with technical teams facing real problems of Urgency and Emergency Health Care.**

Keywords-Health Care System; Big Data; Internet of Things; Agile method and testing; Intelligent Systems; Micro-services Architecture; Cloud Computing; Blockchain; interdisciplinarity; Collaborative problem-based learning.

I. Introduction

This paper tackles the development of an academic project using the Collaborative Interdisciplinary Problem-Based Learning (Co-IPBL). Two issues are emerging in health care as clinicians face the complexities of current patient care: the need for applying new technologies in health care management and the need for these professionals to collaborate with professionals from engineering and computer science background.

Interdisciplinary health care teams with members from many professions usually answer calls, by working together, collaborating, and communicating closely to digitize patients' care [10]-[12].

This research work provides an integration of 3 different courses taught at the Brazilian Aeronautics Institute of Technology (*Instituto Tecnológico de Aeronáutica - ITA*): CE-240 Database Systems Projects, CE-245 Information Technologies, and CE-229 Software Testing. It involved some cooperative work with technical Physicians from Urgent and Emergency Health Care at the Hospital of Clinics from the Faculty of Medicine at the University of São Paulo, Brazil.

It also describes a practical application of collaborative and interdisciplinary concepts, by using the Scrum Agile Method [1]-[3] and Value Engineering. This academic project was driven by ITA to generate expertise on developing, integrating, and managing Emergency and Urgency Health Care in the Hospital of Clinics [4].

This project was named in Portuguese *Soluções Tecnológicas Aplicáveis ao Gerenciamento de Informações Hospitalares Ostensivas com Big Data - STAGIHO-DB*, meaning in English, "Technological Solutions Applicable for Managing Ostensive Hospital Information with Big Data-TSA4MOHIBD". It has considered the development of a Software System, involving Patients, Doctors, Hospitals, and Suppliers, for decision making, by using: Scrum Agile method; Value Engineering; Big Data; Blockchain Hyperledger[9], software quality, reliability, safety, and testability. Scrum Agile Method, Value Engineering, and its best practices were used, in order to develop a computer system to satisfy project requirements in a time frame of just 16 academic weeks.

This TSA4MOHIBD Project [5] was divided into two groups of application: External Regulation and Internal Regulation, by sharing its development among four student teams, which were responsible for developing different functional requirements involving the verification of quality, reliability, safety, and testability.

This research work project was developed by using NodeJs[15] for the development of Java Micro-services (fine-grained services), NoSQL Databases [16] to stored the internal data for the Hospital, Blockchain Hyperledger [9] to stored the electronic health records, Kafka [17] for message exchanging in the common communication data bus, and other emerging technologies. During this collaborative project development, more than 20 students have practiced the roles of Product Owners (POs), Scrum Masters (SMs), and Team Developers (TDs). At the end of this project, a total of 48 User Stories (USs) had been planned to compose the Product Backlog. However, only 36 of them were developed within 3 monthly sprints.At the end of each sprint, reviews and retrospective meetings took place. Moreover, the Acceptance Test Driven Development (ATDD) [6] was applied by generating a minimum, necessary, and sufficient set of artifacts stored at [5].

For each User Story (US), more than one test case and acceptance test were developed. The integration strategy between groups of subsystem components occurred, by using Micro-services, a Commom Data Communication Bus, and Blockchain Hyperledger, allowing information to be available via broadcast to every hospital area and also to the External Regulator named CROSS (named in Portuguese Central de Regulação de Ofertas de Serviços de Saúde and meaning in English the Regulation Center for Health Services Offerings).

An overview of the Urgency and Emergency Care flow is presented in Figure 1.

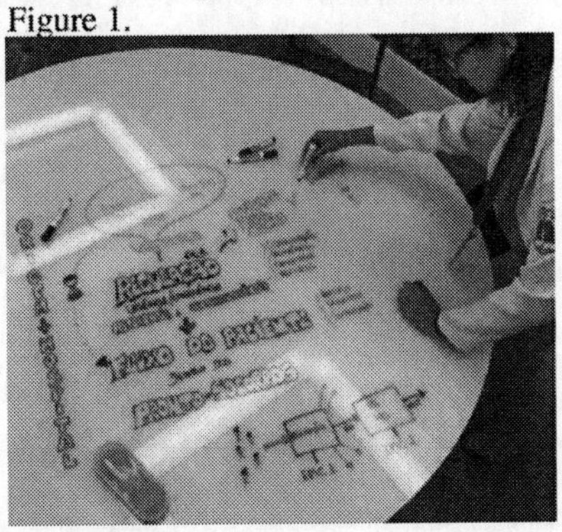

Figure 1. The Emergency and Urgent Care Overview.

In Section II, we describe the attributes of Urgent and Emergency Care at the HCFMUSP. In Section III we present the Proof of Concept and The Proposed System Architecture. In Section IV, we present the specific characteristics of Blockchain Architecture. In Section V, we state our conclusions and suggest possible topics for future research.

II. The Urgency and Emergency Health Care In the HCFMUSP

Before starting the academic year, some students from the Brazilian Aeronautics Institute of Technology (ITA) had a planning meeting with some members of the Emergency Care in the Hospital of Clinics from the Faculty of Medicine at the University of São Paulo (in Portuguese, Hospital da Clínicas da Faculdade de Medicina de São Paulo - HCFMUSP).

On that opportunity, the internal members of the hospital have presented some details of the internal and external regulation and clarified the diagram presented in Figure 1. At that time, there was also an on-site visit to some emergency areas and hospital sectors and it was agreed that some information should be shared with ITA developers, such as students and professors, in order to provide requirements specifications for the next steps of project development.

A. *Regulations*

Regulations of Hospitals and Health Units attending Urgencies and Emergencies are usually carried out by the Health Care Supply Regulatory Center (CROSS). Some urgencies and emergencies are referred to the CROSS by: the Mobile Emergency Response Service (in Portuguese, Serviço de Atendimento Móvel de Urgência - SAMU); the Military Police Operations Center (in Portuguese, Central de Operações Policias Militares - COPOM); the Firefighter Operations Center (in Portuguese, Centro de Operações do Corpo de Bombeiros - COBOM); and/or Health, Secondary Hospitals, and Specialized Hospitals.

It is through the CROSS that the HCFMUSP use to be contacted, in order to respond to urgencies and emergencies. An emergency patient may also arrive by the regular entrance of the HCFMUSP and after contacting the CROSS (usually via email or through the CROSS Web Portal), the HCFMUSP will screen through an Internal Emergency and Emergency Control Center to filter relevant cases for hospital care. Definitions of Urgency and Emergency Health Care are described in Table I.

TABLE I. THE PRINCIPLES OF URGENT AND EMERGENCY CARE

Principles	Resource utilization
Universal Access, Integrality (end-to-end view), Prioritization	Regionalization (Health Offices, Ambulatory Medical Assistance, Hospitals); Hierarchy (The hierarchical division is performed by the health care secretary)

B. *The External Regulation*

The Health Care Secretary of São Paulo understood the regulation as an important tool for the management of public health systems, which has among its objectives the equity of the access implemented through dynamic actions executed in an equitable, orderly, timely and rational way, creating the CROSS, which brings together actions aimed at regulating access in hospitals and outpatient areas, contributing to the integrality of the assistance, providing the adjustment of the available health care supply to the immediate needs of the citizen as described at [13].

Regarding the existing scenario, some characteristics of current Urgent and Emergency Care processes are described on Table II and Table III.

TABLE II. THE EXTERNAL REGULATION - SUMMARY

Current	Details
About Patient Care	Regional units use paper data; dependence on people; patient is directed to the wrong place; lack of resources for care; patient late to the correct location.
About Logistics	Problems mapping criticality versus logistics; manage public versus outsourced ambulances; prioritization versus type of illness; and HCFMUSP also receives patients from other countries (e.g., from Latin America and Africa).
About the Patient Behavior	High demand; everyone wants to come to HCFMUSP; after getting treatment in HC, patient also does not want to return to the regional hospital.
About the Internal Controller	Hospital can not refuse care; the HCFMUSP internal controller evaluates requests and redirect the patient to another Hospital; loss of patient history until arrival at HCFMUSP; data bad described versus delay in the assistance; vacancy zero versus no vacancy in the hospital; internal Controller working as "technical advisor" for the regulator; patients only for evaluation versus how long ambulance needs to wait.
About the Governance	It is unknown, which professionals are in the Health Care Centers; and it is also unknown the availability of beds on Health Care Centers. The regulator has the bed map and can be confirmed with the regulator if the hospital could visualize the availability in other hospitals also. It is unknown, why the Health Center refuses the care requested by the regulator.
About the Standards	There are Laws that regulate how the HCFMUSP Internal Controller should work; there are internal Norms in Hospitals and Health Centers; the Regulator has also specific standards; knowledge from job description of all professionals involved is also required; and there are also norms regulating the external transport of patients.
About Systems Integration	The HCFMUSP accesses the Regulator System, via Portal, and access only requests directed to it; it does not have visibility of care from other health centers; regulator requests are manually checked in the Regulator Portal; regarding the Volume of Orders (as an example, an estimation from the month of June 2017, 2000 applications were received by the Regulator, 540 accepted by the Controller of the USP and out of them, only around 30 could have a vacancy of 0 - which means that the patient has to be accepted; there is no integration between data flows; a typical flow of data on the HC is: Health Units -> Regulator -> HC Internal Controller; a typical flow of data within the HC is: Regulator + Electronic Record at the Reception + Internal Controller; there is a lack of synchronism between actions; the regulator, in the attendance, needs to obtain data from the patient and his illness; and demographic data are needed (from where the patient comes, how he is coming, and when he is arriving).
About the Management of Beds	Treats how to direct the patient in the internal flow (e.g., available beds and specialists); as an example from a Real Scenario, the patient has arrived at 03:00 am to perform an endoscopy, had to stay within the ambulance, mainly because the Hospital did not know of his arrival and can not do the endoscopy. The patient has waited until the morning, because it was not possible to direct the patient in the internal flow; the doctor who was attending the emergency has no contact with the HC and the COBOM system also use to work separately from the HCFMUSP. The COBOM has a manual chart to manage service resources (e.g., where vehicles are located); and the external systems involved in the service are not integrated.

TABLE III. THE EXTERNAL REGULATION - INTERACTIONS

Current	Details
About Data Quality	International Statistical Classification of Diseases and Related Health Problems (ICD) has many groupings and sub-classifications difficult to use in Emergency and Urgency Care; it is necessary to use specific fields to quickly reclassify disease and type of an emergency (e.g., if it is heart attack, trauma, Glasgow (level of consciousness), among others); and Diagnosis Related Groups (DRG) should be used to speed up case classification.
About the Human Factor	The are many problems with reliability of data and the correct use of the systems (e.g., word abbreviations are dependent on the form the clerk expresses).
About the Telemedicine	The doctor attending an emergency does not have contact with the HCFMUSP.
About the Hierarchy	There are some problems in the scheduling of care and diagnostic problems that generate unnecessary referrals to Specialized Hospitals; and problems in the hierarchy, which cause slowness so that the correct patient arrives at the HCFMUSP in the correct time.

C. *The Internal Regulation*

The Internal Regulation is the area responsible in the Hospital for verifying availability to receive a Patient and will also make the contact with the appropriate hospital institute to evaluate if a Patient could be transferred to the Hospital. With regards to the existing scenario, some characteristics of the existing Internal Flow in Urgency and Emergency Care process are described on Table IV.

TABLE IV. THE INTERNAL REGULATION

Current	Details
About the Lobby	It has only one entrance; the stretchers change places; and there is a "virtual bed number" and no "real" fixed number.
About the Identification	There is a bracelet to identify patients; patients who arrive in ambulances use open tokens and are also screened; If a patient is unconscious, he receives a number; and The Manchester Protocol Risk classification is used, which also defines the maximum time for the first service and provides a green / blue classification that does not necessarily leads to the opening of a card. In this case, the patient may be redirected to another region.
About Patient Care	Many patient cares are provided in the lobby; Nurses need to walk between stretchers; doctors can not forget to see the patients; and patients can not fail to take prescribed drugs.
About Patients in the Emergency Room	There is no information about what happens, after the patient passes the entrance door and arrives at the Emergency Room; there are patients who wait for 6 hours in Emergency Room and have not been attended for some reason (e.g., Hospital busy or

Current	Details
	unable to attend); there is only one Patient Card; and there is an assessment of what patient's risk is.
About the Internal Flow of Patients	After screening, patients are referred to an emergency or general medical clinic; and patients may also require evaluation of multiple professionals.
About the Internal Flow of Physicians	There are 11 Medical Teams and sometimes Doctors need to make an assessment of one Patient in the Building of another Institute (e.g., a Neurosurgeon may be in another building evaluating a patient or in a Surgical Center); Medical Specialists move more; and Physicians have mobile, but the signal for mobile does not work well inside buildings that do not have signals with good intensity of the Telephony Operator, but they have a good signal of WiFi. For this reason, Doctors have again used the technology of Pager.
About the Internal Flow of Nurses	Nurses usually stay in more fixed places pre-determined for them.

III. Requirements

A. *The Proof of Concept as an Assigned Mission*

To reduce the scope and complexity of the system to be developed, a mission assigned was developed to the rescue of motorcycle accident victims, mainly because it is a frequent occurrence in the city of São Paulo. On a regular work day, every 15 minutes, the SAMU assists a motorcyclist in the city of São Paulo. Most of victims are not made up of motoboys. Usually, they are drivers who use vehicles (motorbikes) to go to work or are weekend drivers. Rehabilitation of those who are injured is usually time-consuming and laborious, as described below:

- 40\% of motorcycle accident victims need to undergo complex surgeries and long physiotherapy treatments;

- The most serious injuries caused by motorcycle accidents are usually in the skull and spine;

- Most motorcycle riders use the vehicle as transport, only for 2 hours a day, usually to move between home and work place;

Most of them have been injured before;

- Of the total number of accidents initially investigated, 2% resulted in death of motorcyclists;

- Of the total number of injuries: 48% had serious injuries, 17% in the legs and feet; 12% in arms; and 23% had other types of trauma;

- Most of them were discharged immediately after care and only 18% had to be hospitalized; and

- Considering the annual costs, about R$ 100 million are invested by the Orthopedics Institute of the HC, exclusively for the recovery of motorcyclists: "These are patients who, in the first six months of hospitalization, cost about R$ 300 thousands to the Hospital, on surgeries, ICU hospitalizations, occupations of wards, use of medications, among other procedures.

Based on previously reported motorcycle accident data, the development of the TSA4MOHIBD project should be able to provide an adequate management for the control of victim assistance only considering motorcycle accidents, in such a way that:

- Those motorcycle accident victims (PATIENTS) may be appropriately diagnosed, promptly identified and/or attended to;

- PHYSICIANS may have computers and/or computer tools capable of providing preventive and appropriate planning, scheduling, and controlling of motorcycle accident emergency services, for example, identifying the needs of: hospitalization time; procedures; medical teams; procedures for surgery preparations; as well as the availability of operating rooms and Intensive Theraphy Units;

- The HOSPITAL and/or the INTERNAL CONTROLLER shall have computers and/or computer tools capable of using appropriate technologies to provide efficient screening methods, prioritization of care, patient and physician locations within the HOSPITAL, in order to locate, if necessary, other HOSPITALS to attend emergencies of motorcycle accident victims, according to the criticalities and needs from specialized treatments of the PATIENTS;

- HOSPITAL must have adequate computers and/or computer means to collaborate in the process of managing large data flows, involving efficient attendance of injured motorcycle patients, by using appropriate technologies and efficient screening methods for this type of emergency;

- SUPPLIERS of medicines, devices and/or technologies must have appropriate tools to participate in logistics and/or supply process to be used in care and/or care for victims from motorcycle accidents attended by urgency and emergency of HOSPITALS;

- PHYSICIANS and NURSES must have appropriate tools to provide care to victims from motorcycle accidents attended by the urgency and emergency of the HOSPITAL, for example, to identify them from their entrance hall, by verifying and controlling also the movement of the stretchers, according to internal flows of required services;

- Each confirmed case of motorcycle-injured PATIENT can and should generate, within the inventory control of a HOSPITAL, the release of care kits containing materials and medications, according to the size of events. In these cases, in addition to medicines, other supplies can and should be considered important, such as blood bags for transfusions, as accident victims need quick rescue and motorcycle accidents kill from blood loss;

- The population/society should have access to computers and/or computer tools of the System Project involving the TSA4MOHIBD and/or the Real-time TSA4MOHIBD capable of providing appropriate records, management, controls, and governance of resources used in the area of Health Care;

- Public administration must have reliable data to provide a comprehensive situational awareness to support decision making for accidents and/or crises, involving motorcycle accidents.

B. *The Proposed System Architecture*

In order to provide appropriate speed in the communication with the Regulator and also to allow the

Regulator to know in advance the number of bed vacancy in the Hospital, it is suggested that the communication between the Regulator and the Hospital works similarly to the AirBnB model. Then, the hospital will publish in a data bus communication vacancy, physicians, and specialists available and also the Regulator will publish a request for a patient to be attended and its initial conditions. On top of that, it will run an Artificial Intelligence algorithm to verify that the Regulator needs a Patient to be treated and will also match the required care with the Hospital that has vacancy to receive the Patient. The Artificial Intelligence algorithm, after finding the appropriate Hospital, will place in the same data bus a message to the Hospital. Some External Flow Architecture Details are shown in Figure 2.

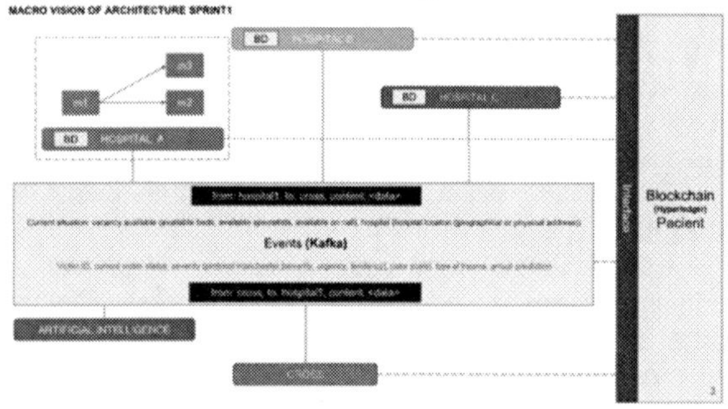

Figure 2. The External Flow Architecture.

In the Hospital at the Internal Regulator, the operator will analyze the request and through the application system he will place a message in the Data Bus, by informing to Artificial Intelligence algorithm that the Patient was accepted and will inform straight the Urgency Care Unit that a Patient will arrive, also informing the date and time of the estimated arrival. The patient information will be available in the Blockchain Hyperledger, and then, data from the CROSS and also data about the Patient will be internally matched in the Hospital.

Some important details about how it will work will also be presented in the Blockchain Architecture section. From that point onwards, the planning for Patient Care will be started prior to the Patient arrival. When the Patient arrives the technical team, the bed, and the required examination and health care steps will proceed as per suggested planning. After acceptance from the Internal Controller, the intelligence of the system will place a message to the Regulator, by informing that the Patient was accepted by the HCFMUSP. Some Internal Flow Architecture Details are shown in Figure 3.

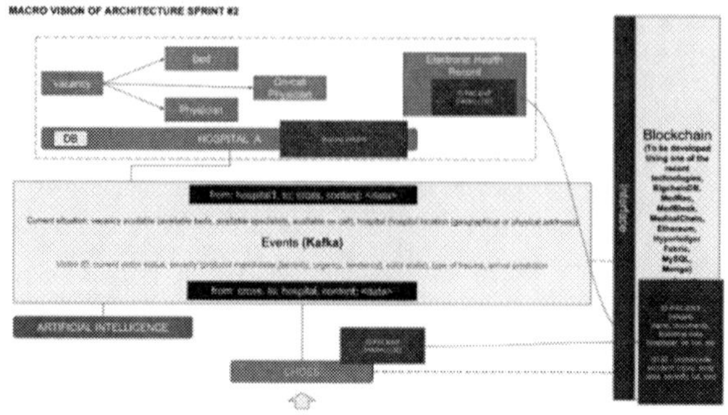

Figure 3. The Internal Controller Flow Architecture.

After a Patient arrived at the Hospital, his Electronic Health Record could be read by any Institute from inside of the HCFMUSP, and information about patient care steps, as all the current bed management in the Hospital, would be presented in a dashboard that could be available for the governance team, by physicians and nurses looking at the next steps of the Patient Care. Some internal management information are shown in Figure 4.

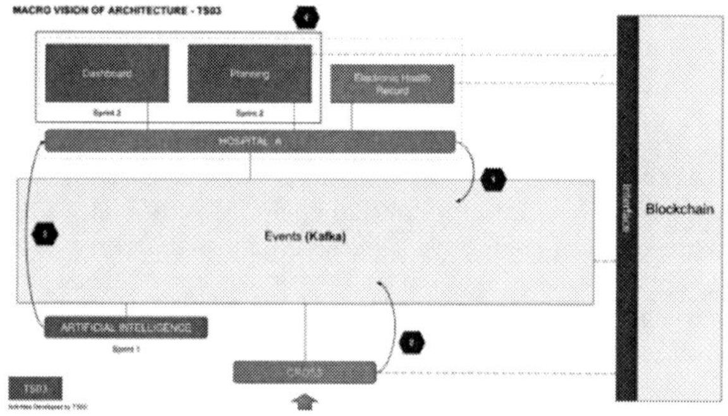

Figure 4. The Dashboard for Patient Care.

IV. THE BLOCKCHAIN ARCHITECTURE

A. *Blockchain Applications in Health Care*

Blockchain technology and smart contracts have a variety of application in Health Care and, as recently reported, there are multiple advantages, such as a common database of health information that doctors and providers could access, no matter what electronic medical system they use, higher security and privacy, less admin time for doctors, so there is more time to spend on patient care, and even better sharing of research results to facilitate new drug and treatment therapies for disease, as recently mentioned by a research published by Forbes [7].

In the open-source landscape map for healthcare-related blockchain published in GitHub [8], there are multiple companies in the early stage of applying this technology as shown in Figure 5.

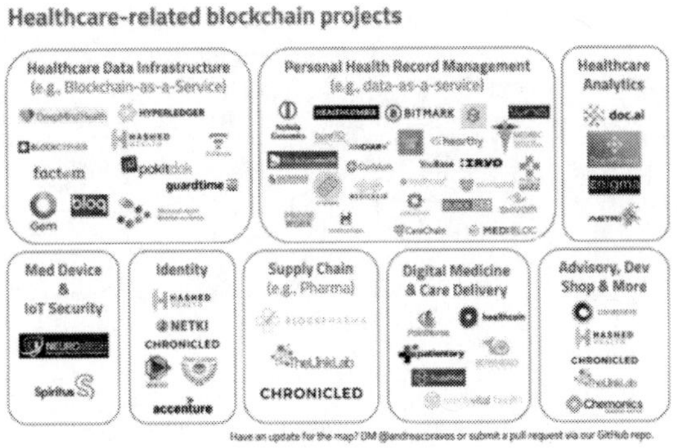

Figure 5. The open-source landscape map for healthcare-related blockchain.

The Blockchain proposed for the Urgency and Emergency Care at the HCFMUSP explores how Blockchain Hyperledger [9][14] and smart contracts could be used to provide an interesting and innovative way to keep references of the Patient data, since the occurrence of the emergency until the completion of Patient treatment in the Hospital.

To do this, first we discuss the need of two separate and private blockchain networks and then, we propose an architecture that is able to use those different networks applied to the motorcycle accident Proof of Concept.

B. The Blockchain Proposal for the HCFMUSP

For the Urgency and Emergency Care at the HCFMUSP, our proposal is to use two separate Blockchain networks: one for Patient and other for Attendance.

The Blockchain Patient network has overall patient information and is a private network with information that can be accessed by the CROSS and any other Institution that would like in the future to access Patient Identification (e.g., Single Health System, in Portuguese, named Sistema Único de Saúde - SUS).

The Blockchain Attendance network has detailed patient information and all the heath care details performed by the Hospital. And it is a private network with information that can be accessed only by the Hospital and internal institutes. For future work, examination details could be also stored in this Blockchain network. The main benefit of isolating patient's data from patient's own care is to provide data safety, since confidential information will be managed only by the hospital. The indirect benefit is to allow that two different groups of students learning Blockchain could also learn separately and then, the integration has worked smoothly during the Sprint 3 of the TSA4MOHIBD project, focusing in the Integration.

The Blockchain Hyperledger implementation also makes use of encapsulated micro-services allowing smooth funcionalities' integrations, which were developed during Sprint 1, focusing in the External Flow implementation, and Sprint2, focusing in the Internal Flow Implementation. The steps followed to assist a patient using the Blockchain Hyperledger architecture are shown in Figure 6, on Table V and Table VI.

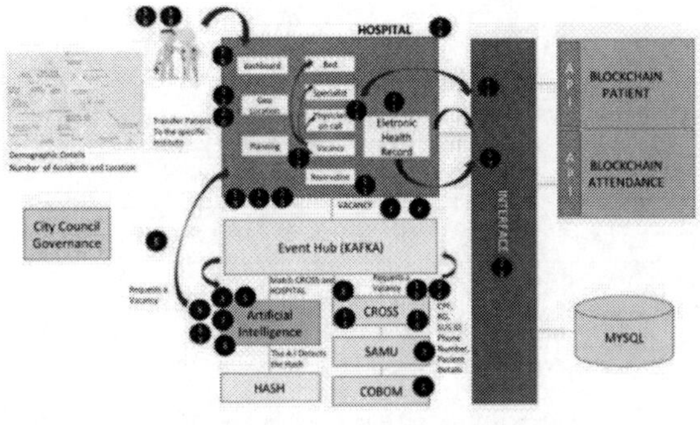

Figure 6. The Architecture for the Urgency and Emergency Patient Care.

TABLE V. THE STEPS FOR THE URGENT AND EMERGENCY PATIENT CARE – EXTERNAL FLOW

Step	Details
1	The fire department team receives notification of an accident (via process, not system implementation), by updating the occurrence of 14:17 Auto x Moto, Rua Coronel João Cabanas, 650 - Grajaú, 1 vehicle, victim rescued by SAMU # 193R. 4:14 PM - 27 May 2018
2	The SAMU, in contact with the CROSS, informs the details about the accident and the patient. The name of the patient is informed as well as that the biker's legs, ankles, and feet have been affected (via process, not via implementation system).
3	The CROSS requests a slot on the message data bus. With the message bus, it was created an INTELLIGENCE that reads CROSS requests and messages that the HOSPITAL generates checking that hospitals have beds available for the care.
4	Hospitals, including the HCFMUSP, post a message every 15 minutes, reporting the total available vacancies and there are 3 vacancies in the Emergency and Central Institute. Current situation: vacancy available (available beds, available specialists, available on call), hospital (hospital location (geographical or physical address))
5	The INTELLIGENCE reads the message data bus and verifies that the HCFMUSP has a vacancy available and sends a message directly to the HCFMUSP, informing patient's data and his current situation. Victim ID, current victim status, severity (from the manchester protocol, color scale), type of trauma, and arrival prediction).
6	Information about the accident region is also shared with the CROSS in the message data bus. PATIENT ID (HASH) name, CPF, RG, documents (SUS), latitude, longitude for example: id132 - (motorcycle accident, injury, body area, severity, lat, lon) Rua Coronel João Cabanas, 650 - Grajaú.
7	The victim is taken to the Hospital by the SAMU ambulance (The communication with the SAMU occurs via the process, not through the system).
8	At the HCFMUSP, the Control Planner makes the consultation to specialists, beds, and through demographic data verifying how long the PATIENT will arrive at the HC, and that the transportation will be made by SAMU.
9	Upon verification by the Controlling Party, a message is posted by INTELLIGENCE on the bus to the CROSS, confirming the acceptance of the procedure TS03-US103 PATIENT. If the CONTROLLING PLANT did not accept the PATIENT, the INTELLIGENCE would verify the vacancy in another HOSPITAL (This is a recommendation, but not implemented yet).
10	The CROSS confirms to the SAMU that the PATIENT will be directed to the HCFMUSP (implemented via process, not via system yet).

Step	Details
11	Upon confirmation of the PATIENT by the Internal Controller, the Internal Controller also advises the Emergency Room to prepare the internal flow to receive the PATIENT.

TABLE VI. THE STEPS FOR THE URGENT AND EMERGENCY PATIENT CARE – INTERNAL FLOW

Step	Details
12	In the Emergency Room, the internal flow of activities begins to prepare care. PATIENT data, via blockchain, are received and some actions for the reservation are initiated. The vacancy is reserved. The bed is reserved in procedure TS01-US299b and a physician is booked.
13	Service planning starts, Exams, Operating room. Patient's travel time to the Hospital areas are also calculated and estimated.
14	The Internal CONTROLLER shows the situation of the HOSPITAL after reserving the bed, also verifying available specialists, available beds, and the Physician on call. The Emergency Dashboard also provides an up-to-date view upon reservation and service planning.
15	The CROSS may request other vacancies, to refer other patients according to the occurrences, if necessary.
16	PATIENT arrives at the HCFMUSP.
17	The Emergency Unit, through the data of the PATIENT locate in the BLOCKCHAIN, finds the his Electronic Health Record. / get (getAll) / get / {hash} (getByHash).
18	The necessary identification is made, by using QR Code bracelets (This is also a recommendation, not implemented yet).
19	All PATIENTS care are performed according to pre-planning.
20	According to results from tests, the PATIENT will need surgery by the orthopedic team, he is not at risk, and his transfer can be done to the Orthopedics and Traumatology Institute - OTI (This is also a recommendation not implemented yet).
21	The PATIENT remains in URGENCY and EMERGENCY for one day, and through the internal flow he is transferred the next day to the OTI.
22	PATIENT records are updated through the blockchain and can be consulted by the OTI.
23	After the transfer, the vacancy is made available at the Urgency and Emergency of the Central Institute.
24	New services follow the same flow for receiving motorcycle accident victims in the city of São Paulo. According to some OTI statistics, every 15 minutes, a motorcyclist suffers an accident in the City of São Paulo.

C. *The Blockchain Implementation*

For the Urgency and Emergency Care at the HCFMUSP, our proposal is to use two separate Blockchain networks: one for Patient and other for Attendance.

For the implementation, it was identified the four main flows for the Blockchain Hyperledger integration. The following details are shown in Figure 7.

- Register Assets (e.g Physicians, Hospitals);
- Authorize a PATIENT Care;
- Perform PATIENT Care; and
- Register information from the PATIENT Care.

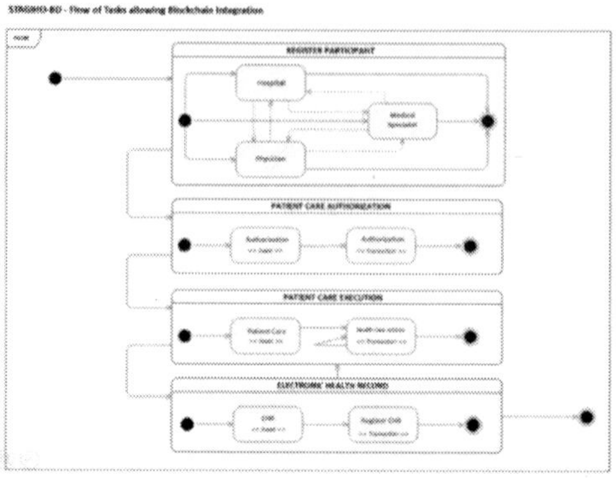

Figure 7. Some Blockchain Integration Activities.

For the authorization in the Blockchain, two flows were identified: the first one to authorize Assets and the second to authorize and finalize Patient Care. Some details are shown in Figure 8.

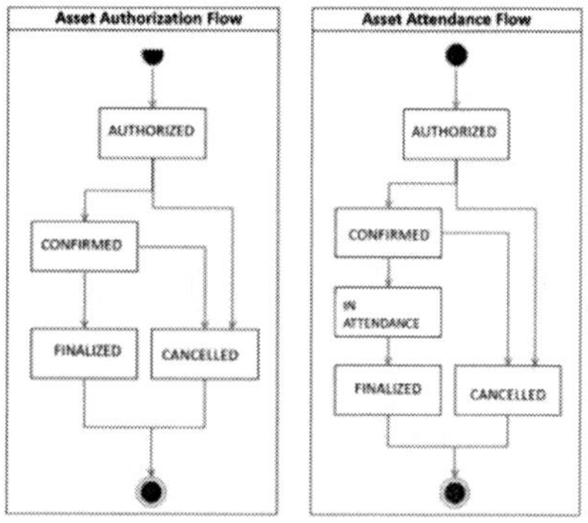

Figure 8. Some Blockchain Authorization Activities.

Some Graphical Interfaces are shown in Figure 9 and Figure 10.

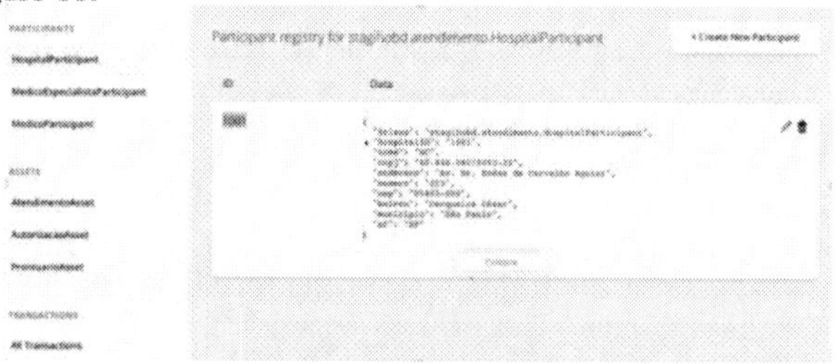

Figure 9. The Hospital Participant.

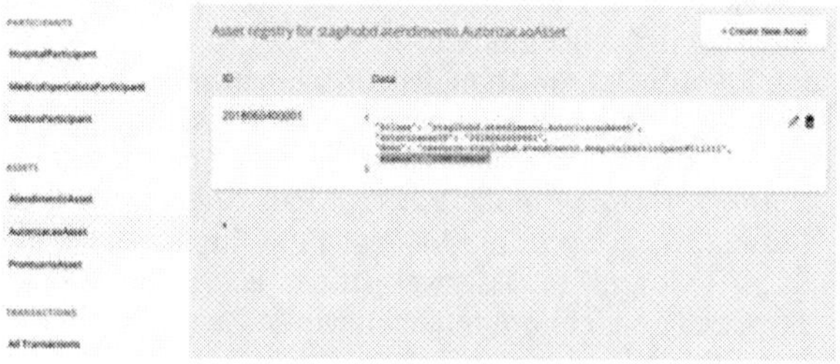

Figure 10. The Patient Authorization.

V. Conclusion

This paper aimed to describe the development of an academic interdisciplinary project using Scrum agile method and its best practices, in order to develop a prototype for a Proof of Concept (PoC), by using a Computer System based on Big Data, Blockchain Hyperledger, Micro-services, and other emerging technologies applied to Urgency and Emergency Care.

This academic research project was named in Portuguese as "*Soluções Tecnológicas Aplicáveis ao Gerenciamento de Informações Hospitalares Ostensivas com Big Data - STAGIHO-DB*", meaning in English, "Technological Solutions Applicable for the Management of Ostensive Hospital Information with Big Data - TSA4MOHIBD", a Computer System based on Big Data, Blockchain Hyperledger, Micro-services, and other emerging technologies for governmental organization and private sector.

The purpose of this system was to aggregate data and integrate sectors such as External and Internal Regulations through its PATIENTS, HOSPITALS, PHYSICIANS, and HEALTH SUPPLIERS, for the decision making process related to Urgency and Emergency Care, involving motorcycle accidents. The TSA4MOHIBD project was developed by students from three different Computer Science courses taught at the Brazilian Aeronautics Institute of Technology (*Instituto Tecnológico de Aeronáutica – ITA*), on the 1st Semester of 2018.

A. Specific Conclusions

The use of interdisciplinarity in 3 courses of Computer Science has worked as expected, since students were able to know how to work in teams to successfully develop a complex computer system.

The cloud computing environment has been widely used by students to enable collaborative work from distance, by using remote meetings, personal websites, and an official project website.

The Scrum framework has been adapted to the reality of the interdisciplinary academic environment of ITA, helping the entire team of more than 20 students to offer value to stakeholders at the end of each sprint and also at the end of this project.

The application of Test Driven Development (TDD) and Acceptance Testing Driven Development (ATDD) techniques in the project was closely related to the interdisciplinary approach adopted, since acceptance tests were created by CE-229 Software Testing course students, while the Blockchain and NodeJS applications were implemented by CE-240 Database System Project and CE-245 Information Technologies course students.

The Blockchain Hyperledger, NodeJs, MongoDB, and MySQL Databases were hosted on the AWS Cloud services and have represented the main tools applied for integrating services from External and Internal Regulations.

The main results obtained from the use of the TSA4MOHIBD project prototype were successful.

Its operating logic was established and all teams were able to perform development integration, by defining and accomplishing the phases of an Assigned Mission, mapping User Stories to functionalities for the External and Internal regulations integration, which variables and detailed characteristics would be changed as inputs and/or outputs.

At the end of this project, in just 17 weeks, it was possible to demonstrate the building of the Collaborative Interdisciplinary Project TSA4MOHIBD, without completeness, but following a model with quality, reliability, safety, testability, norms, and standards applicable to a product of this nature.

Finally, students have presented the TSA4MOHIBD Academic Project Prototype, as the final project for their courses, as a Proof of Concept (PoC) to professors, entrepreneurs, and some invited guests from industry and academia.

B. General Conclusions

The academic development of a critical intelligent system is a rewarding experience that can be used in different undergrad and graduate courses.

The use of interdisciplinarity, Blockchain Hyperledger, cloud computing, and agile methods seems to be an interesting novel and exciting way to achieve academic goals, in just one semester of 17 weeks and can also be extended to other knowledge domains.

It is possible to integrate products generated with Blockchain Hyperlegder, from different teams and functional segments, such as the Internal and External Regulation, with different technologies for example Micro-services, NodeJs, MongoDB and MySQL Databases, from a minimal organization between teams, by defining separated Blockchain networks with medical ostensive data to be exchanged between each Blockchain network, allowing collective planning among all involved.

This integration can be extended to participants, running on different machines integrated through the Blockchain Hyperledger Patient network.

Hospitals can be considered ledgers and, as proposed in this architecture, can have an specific Blockchain Hyperledger Attendance network were specific Health Care information can be securely and safely stored.

C. Recommendations

It is strongly recommended to align expectations and results that may be compromised and quickly adjusted to review deliverables, when working with emerging technologies. This cycle, in the area of computing science, should be repeated all the time we have to deal with new technologies. It is important to have on the team participants who will face the challenge of learning and preparing a legacy.

It is also fundamental to have participants in the team that could identify in advance where the team could fail with the new technology, proposing improvements and allowing the team to repositioning itself to deliver what is agreed in consensus in the appropriate time. Tutorials prepared by the team during the Blockchain Hyperlegder learning process can be used to demonstrate for all team members to quickly acquire knowledge about this new technology.

This very important legacy from teams will help the next teams to face challenges of using new technologies. It is recommended the continuation of this Project, by starting from what has already been done, possible to obtain and execute, within the courses on the next semesters, on new Sprints, generating the possibility of increasing completeness.

D. *Future Work*

It is suggested that the process used in this TSA4MOHIBD academic project prototype can be extended to other Blockchain Hyperledger projects and predictive systems, in order to improve estimation of efforts and resources to attend Urgency and Emergency Care.

It is also suggested the use of some simulation processes to measure Urgency and Emergency Care with and without the use of Blockchain Hyperledger supporting health management.

Finally, for future work, it is suggested to expand some cooperation among the ITA, hospitals, innovation foundations, medical suppliers, industries and public and private enterprises, in order to get a selection of academic projects aligned to updated needs from the market.

ACKNOWLEDGMENT

The authors would like to thank the Hospital of Clinics from The Faculty of Medicine at The University of São Paulo, the Brazilian Aeronautics Institute of Technology, the Ecossistema Negócios Digitais Ltda for its finantial support and scholarships, and The Casimiro Montenegro Filho Foundation (FCMF) for their support, during the development of this TSA4MOHIBD Project.

REFERENCES

[1] J. Sutherland, "SCRUM Handbook", Scrum Training Institute Press, 2017

[2] D. Cohen et al., "An Introduction to Agile Methods", Fraunhofer Centerfor Experimental Software Engineering, ADVANCES IN COMPUTERS,VOL. 62., 2004

[3] M. Cohn, "Succeeding with agile: Software development using Scrum",1st Edition, Pearson Education, Inc, 2010

[4] FMUSP, "Medical School of São Paulo", 2018, accessed from http://www.fm.usp.br/fmusp/portal/ in June 10, 2018.

[5] TSA4MOHIBD Project, "Technological Solutions Applicable for theManagement of Ostensive Hospital Information with Big Data", 2018, accessed from https://sites.google.com/site/projetointerdisciplinar2018/ in June 10, 2018.

[6] K. Pugh, "Lean-Agile Acceptance Test-Driven Development: Better Soft-ware Through Collaboration", Addison-Wesley, ISBN 978-0321714084, 2011

[7] Forbes, "This is Why Blockchain will Transform HealthCare", 2017, accessed from https://www.forbes.com/sites/bernardmarr/2017/11/29/this-is-why-blockchains-will-transform-healthcare/13be90781ebe in June 10, 2018.

[8] GitHub, "Open-source landscape map for healthcare-related blockchain", 2018 accessed from https://github.com/acoravos/healthcare-blockchains in June 10, 2018.

[9] Linux Foundation Projects, "Blockchain Hyperledger", 2018 accessed from https://www.hyperledger.org/ in June 10, 2018.

[10] D. A. Silva et al.,"Health Care Information Systems: a Crisis Approach", In 15th International Conference on Information Technology: NewGenerations (ITNG 2018), Las Vegas, 2018

[11] D. A. Silva et al., "Health Care Transformation: An Academic Applica-tion System Case Study", In 10TH IFAC Symposium on Biological andMedical Systems - International Federation of Automatic Control (IFACBMS 2018), São Paulo, Brazil, 2018

[12] J. C. Martins et al., "Using Big Data, Internet of Things, and Agile for Crises Management", In 14th International Conference on InformationTechnology: New Generations (ITNG 2017), Las Vegas, US, 2017

[13] Cross, "Health Care Supply Regulatory Center", 2018, accessed from http://www.cross.saude.sp.gov.br/ in June 10, 2018.

[14] [14] A. Conceicao, F. Silva, V. Rocha, A. Locoro, J. Barguil, "EletronicHealth Records Using Blockchain", XXXVI Brazilian Symposium on Computer Networks and Distributed Systems (SBRC 2018), 2018, accessed from http://www.sbrc2018.ufscar.br/wp-content/uploads/2018/04/07-181717-1.pdf in June 10, 2018.

[15] Linux Foundation Projects, "Node.JS Foundation", 2018, accessed from https://nodejs.org/en/ in 10.June 2018.

[16] Apache Kafka, "Apache Kafka Distributed Stream Platform", 2018,accessed from http://kafka.apache.org/

[17] MongoDB, "MongoDB", 2018, accessed from https://www.mongodb.com/

xAudit: Auditing Representation in XBRL Based Documents

Allison Ramon Araújo de Santana[1], Paulo Caetano da Silva[1], Márcio A. Pereira da Silva[2], Maurício Codesso[3]
PPGCOMP – Universidade Salvador (UNIFACS) [1], Center for Informatics, Federal University of Pernambuco[2],
Universidade Federal de Santa Catarina[3], Brazil
E-mail: paulo.caetano@unifacs.com, allison-valente@hotmail.com, marcio.alexandre83@gmail.com, mmcodesso@gmail.com

***Abstract* — Most financial documents are presented to governments and governors in computer language (e.g., XBRL). Information acquired from said reports should be free from faults, omissions and fraud, making it trustworthy to the point of supporting strategic decisions by the organizations that receive them. Although XBRL technologies present financial data and its accounting semantics, the auditing techniques used (which make this data even more trustworthy) are not stored or listed in the XBRL taxonomies. This fact makes it difficult to perform the auditing of these files, given that it's up to the auditor to apply the concepts of auditing manually, without the assistance of the automated auditing process. With the continuous auditing it's more and more possible to avoid the recidivism of fraud or even to identify it more quickly. Despite many auditing operations being performed under the XBRL perspective, it has not yet been defined a standard for the auditing of XBRL files. This paper proposes the establishment of a link database (*Linkbase,* in XLINK language), based on the XBRL specifications, which has been named xAudit, for the listing and storing of auditing techniques in XBRL taxonomies. To do so, a solution has been created, based on the XBRL definitions and auditing-specific regulations. Using xAudit, people try to solve the shortage for a standard for XBRL auditing. Some important points of the auditing process are raised in the present article. Using xAudit, it's expected that organizations can achieve improved results, real-time verification and accurate data analysis.**

Keywords-Continuous Auditing; Auditing Standards; XBRL; xAudit.

I. Introduction

Financial reports are meant to provide useful information for the interested sides involved in an organization or its processes. All information acquired from these reports should be free from mistakes, omissions and fraud, making it trustworthy to the point of supporting strategic decisions by the organizations that receive them [1].

Auditing is a systematic process, documented and independent for the acquirement of evidence (registers, fact submission or other information) that aim to verify the satisfactory meeting of the defined criteria (set of policies, procedures or requirements) [2].

Standardizing is one of the factors that contribute for a suitable auditing, given that, with non-standardized data, it's up to the auditor to manually "clean" the data so the automated auditing process can take place [1].

XBRL technology has been increasingly utilized by national and international financial systems, such as SICONFI system, of the National Treasury Secretariat of Brazil [13]. In 2009, the American Securities and Exchange Commission (SEC), started demanding for companies of local or foreign capital, with operations in the country, to disclose their financial reports in XBRL format [3]. In March of 2017, an update on their internal systems enabled public companies to use the XBRL format for the emission of financial statements, as well [4]. The Organisation for Economic Cooperation and Development (OECD) recommends that tax administrators take into consideration data formatting that allows for the use of automated auditing, in order to minimize potential costs for the interested sides. To that effect, the Organisation acknowledges in particular the use of open financial data standards, such as XBRL and XBRL GL [5].

Many auditing operations have been built on the XBRL perspective, such as the Forensic LMDQL [6]. In February 4th, 2015, the XBRL International [7] organized a meeting to take a standing regarding the drafting of a proposal to be sent to members of the international normalization committee [8] to establish an International Standard (ISO) for auditing data with commercial and governmental usage, for both internal and external auditing. Several relevant decrees and regulations of international, national and regional levels were presented, but the project wasn't approved nonetheless, given the proposal hadn't taken into consideration several standards known to the committee, e.g., OECD Standard Audit File – Tax, United Nations auditing regulations [14], Swedish SIE [15], Dutch Auditfile Financieel [16], Object Management Group's GL Facility and Open Application Group's (OAGIS). Some aspects were pointed out to guide the improvement of the standardizing proposal, such as a more accurate definition of terms deemed vague and/or indeterminate [5], and so a new evaluation of the project is awaited anytime soon.

Based on this scenario, as there is no agreement on which standard to be used or even a regulation as basis for the execution of the auditing process, it is understood that there's a need for a generic standard for the representation of different auditing techniques, contributing to the implementation of auditing on XBRL reports. Therefore, an extension of the XBRL 2.1 is proposed, named xAudit, to assist in this process. Said extension is based on XBRL standards, such as Generic Links [17], so that it is a solution consistent with the syntactic and semantic structure of XBRL. xAudit can be a new and useful tool to aid and automate the auditing process in XBRL-formatted files.

This work is divided in five sessions, in the session I The Introduction, in the session II Theoretical Foundation, in the session III Correlated Works, in the session VI xAudit Specification end session V Conclusion, Limitations and Future Works.

II. THEORETICAL FOUNDATION

This session presents the concepts of *XBRL* and *Continuous Audit*.

A. XBRL

XBRL, is and open international standard, based on XML (Extensible Markup Language), meant for the exchange of business information. XBRL has its specifications defined by the XBRL International Consortium [18], being based on the technological standards of W3C [19]. XBRL is already present in many countries, including The United States, Japan, Korea, United Kingdom, Australia, Denmark, Argentina, France, China, India, Ireland, Italy, New Zealand and Brazil [9].

The XBRL 2.1 specification is formed by two main elements: taxonomy and instance document. In taxonomy, the terms representing financial concepts are described, i.e., the vocabulary that will be used in the instance document, as well as the relations between said terms, the description and classification of the business. The semantics and syntax of the financial information is described in the taxonomy. On the other hand, the instance document contains the financial data and the description of its textual elements. An instance document may be connected to more than one taxonomy at once, as long as it uses elements described in them. The set of these two elements, instance document and taxonomy, is what composes XBRL documents [10].

An XBRL document can be generated from data acquired from many sources, including, but not restricted to: XML documents, manual inputs and databases. The distribution of an XBRL document can be executed in a way that integrates it in several different formats (HTML, PDF, Word RTF) or even in a database [10]. Receiving documents in various formats, converting them into and auditable format (XBRL) favors the process of acquiring evidence generated in all organizational levels, in order to increase even further the amount for analysis or the range of the auditing. In addition, distributing the information in different formats allow even more integration between different software platforms.

With a standardized representation, the XBRL facilitates the acquisition of trustworthy and accurate data, providing a better analysis of the risk of the transaction, control mitigation and operational efficiency [10].

Financial information of the kind distributed through XBRL reports must be trustworthy, given that it is essential for the daily routine of organizations, as decisions about investments and credit, or even strategic organizational planning, are made based on it [1].

B. Continuous Auditing

In the auditing process, the evidence is acquired and presented in conclusive reports, in a way that points out aspects that require improvements, as well as stresses unconformities, aiming to solve their original cause, thus avoiding recurrence.

In traditional auditing, the process tends to be slow, especially because of aggravating effects such as the sample limitation or even the manual procedures. Generally, the market acts dynamically and, if the rhythm of the auditing is slower, the decision-making, most of the time, tends to be delayed, inducing a loss of competitive edge, increased costs and decreased productivity [10].

In the paradigm of traditional auditing, the data is periodically verified and, as an outcome, faults, fraud or omissions can last long periods without being detected by an auditing or because of it [1].

Continuous auditing takes place more frequently or even continuously. In this process, the monitoring of controls and operations in a shorter time lapse allow for the auditor to detect the deviations faster and more efficiently, contributing for a timely, adequate response [1].

The continuous auditing process becomes even more efficient with the use of technology and automation Improved methods make significant increases in efficiency of an auditing process more likely to happen, as it allow for more frequent auditings, making the information more reliable and readily available [1].

The monitoring and continuous auditing processes integrated with XBRL technology allow for data, in the operational level, to be defined in a single way, being then read, interpreted and analyzed in real time. A standardized representation favors a more trustworthy and efficient data collection, to achieve a higher capacity of data analysis, being able to account for negotiation risks, efficiency and operational control, meeting of determinations and demand verification in a shorter time [10].

For the present work, auditing techniques have been applied to enable the identification and responsibilization of the auditor, definition of context of the auditing to be executed, type and method of the auditing, conformity, action management, activities and processes scheduling, among others. Said techniques are available for reference in Section IV (xAudit Specification).

III. CORRELATED WORKS

The number of articles produced in Brazil about XBRL is not high. The main focuses of research, discussion and propagation of XBRL in Brazil are the TECSI-USP (Laboratory of Technology and Information Systems) coordinated by Dr. Edson Luiz Riccio, and the Group of Research in Software Engineering and Applications (GESA) [20] [21], laboratory of the master's in Systems and Computing from UNIFACS (Salvador University), coordinated by professor Dr. Paulo Caetano da Silva (Farias, 2014). The former, TECSI, operates exclusively in the area of business, while the latter, GESA, develops works based on XBRL technology, both in the areas of business and Information Technology.

Regulations and standards are defined in order to adapt, from the existing taxonomies, the needs of each country and region [5]. A few studies were pointed, regarding topics like the benefits and challenges of XBRL in Brazil; data models for federal organizations; continuous auditing, however not necessarily about XBRL; implications of XBRL in the process of continuous auditing.

It is noticed the existence of standards that enable data extraction from accountability systems, for example the standards developed by American Institute of Certified

Public Accountants (AICPA), with the goal of generating files that are fit for auditing [11].

Due to the difficulty in finding national and international researches about auditing in XBRL files, it is hoped that xAudit fills this gap, in order to instigate the topic in the academic community and create a generic representation for auditing techniques in XBRL-formatted data, thus allowing for the automation of auditing processes in XBRL documents, and its use in public and private institutions.

IV. xAUDIT SPECIFICATION

Taking into account the existence of auditing regulations, such as NBR ISO 19011 (Guidelines for the auditing of quality and/or environmental management systems) [2], and the Data Standard for Auditing, proposed by American Institute of Certified Public Accountants (AICPA) [3], it was sought, in this work, to analyze these documents in order to identify essential terminology and concepts for an auditing process that, put together and adjusted, could create a standard to be used jointly with XBRL technology for Continuous Auditing, in this case, the xAudit.

In Figure 1, it is represented the set of documents used as basis for the theoretical foundation of xAudit, as well as its relationship with XBRL technology.

Figure 1. xAudit.

To enable the execution of continuous auditing in XBRL files, a set of terms to be annexed to the xAudit taxonomy has been defined, which in turn represents part of the auditing process.

In order for an auditing to take place, it is required that a range, criteria, reference regulations and evidence to be analyzed are defined. Aiming to meet the organizational schedule in what regards the period and scope of the audited processes, it is proposed the representation og an auditing plan, containing information, such as frequency, kind of auditing and responsible parts [2].

This way, XBRL instances for certain processes may be analyzed based on the established criteria. The conformity analysis may also be executed, and log files generated, which will be basis for the composition of the recommendation report of the auditing. Taking into account the improvements pointed out, action plans can be laid out for monitoring the steps taken as a result of the auditing.

In Figure 2, an UML representation of xAudit can be seen. Following that, its elements are described.

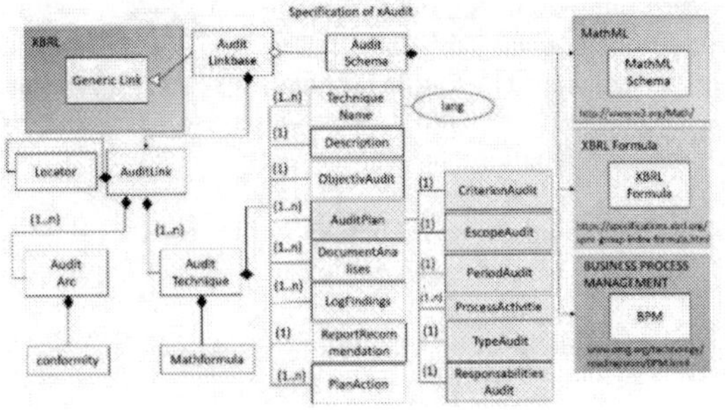

Figure 2. UML representation of xAudit.

Given that business auditing techniques can be mathematically represented, this work also proposes the interconnection between xAudit and XBRL technologies, such as XBRL Formula and MathML, which represent documents of business regulations and mathematical calculations, respectively. It's also presented in this work an XBRL Linkbase, as an xAudit element, to establish the connection between the technologies, as illustrated by Figure 3.

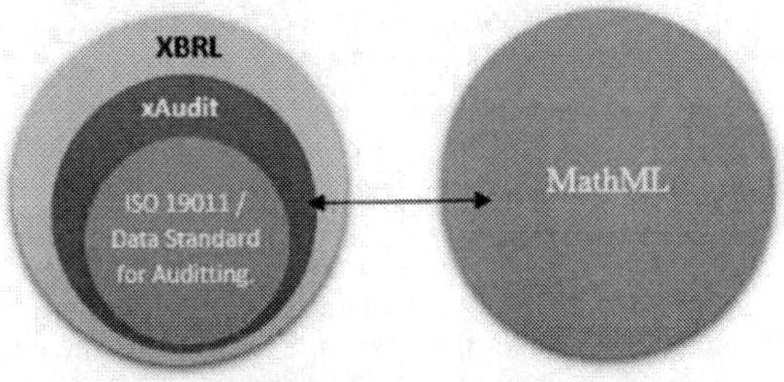

Figure 3. Connection Between The Technologies.

The specific elements for the composition of xAudit are described below.

A. *Audit Schema*

The xAudit schema file defines the elements that can be part of the semantic representation of the auditing technique. These elements are based on XBRL taxonomy.

B. *Audit Linkbase*

The file <Audit Linkbase> is a document that stores the representation of the auditing technique and its connections with the business elements. This file is an specialization of the Generic Link specification (XBRL Inc., 2009), which has been devised to extend XBRL to new semantics.

In this file (Audit Linkbase), the taxonomist expresses the elements that represent the auditing technique. This representation is based on the elements contained in the xAudit schema file, which is explained below:

1) Audit Link

The element <AuditLink> represents a set of interconnected elements. The subelements of <AuditLink> are (i) Locator [12], which locates elements in the XBRL taxonomy (ii) Resource [12], specified to represent a resource to be used by the taxonomist and (iii) Arc [12], which establishes a connection arc between the previous elements. AuditLink may contain several Locators, Resources and Arcs.

1.1) Audit Technique

The element <AuditTechnique> represents the auditing technique. Ten children elements have been specified for its formal representation:

1.1.1) TechniqueName

The element <TechniqueName> describes the name of the applied auditing technique.

1.1.2) Description

The element <Description> represents the theoretical concept of the technique represented in the file. This description has to be in natural language, as expressed in the *Lang* attribute.

1.1.3) Mathformula

The element <Mathformula> represents a mathematical formula that formalizes the respective auditing technique, based on the elements defined in the xAudit schema file.

1.1.4) ObjectiveAudit

The element <ObjectiveAudit> determines the objective of the auditing that will be executed. Three different objectives were defined, divided by level:

- Level 1: <Routine Check> (Detect routine transaction irregularities that stand out);
- Level 2: <Conformity Check> (Aims to compare the set criteria with collected evidence);
- Level 3: <Reanalysis check> (Redo the auditing process in order to verify the consistency of the collected data).

1.1.5) Audit Plan

The element <AuditPlan> defines details that facilitate the understanding between the involved parts, in such a way that reflects the complexity of the auditing, just as much as it enables the process. Composed by the elements: <CriterionAudit>, <EscopeAudit>, <PeriodAudit>, <ProcesseActivitie>, <TypeAudit> e <ResponsabilitiesAudit>, described below:

1.1.5.1) CriterionAudit

The element <CriterionAudit> is used as reference for ascertaining of conformity. It describes the regulations and regulatory items to be used as criteria. (EX: 1: NBC TA 230_– AUDITING DOCUMENT - CFC, items 10 and 11, 2: NBC TA 530 – AUDITING SAMPLING, items 5 and 6);

1.1.5.2) EscopeAudit

The element <EscopeAudit> describes the scope and limits of the auditing that will be executed, in a way that defines what hierarchical or documental levels will be audited.

1.1.5.3 PeriodAudit

<PeriodAudit> defines the period in which the audit will take place, as well as the schedule for its execution.

1.1.5.4) ProcessActivitie

<ProcessActivitie> defines the processes or activities that will go through documental analysis.

1.1.5.5) TypeAudit

<TypeAudit> determines if the auditing process will be carried out by an internal or external (independent) team, about the audited organization.

1.1.5.6) ResponsabilitiesAudit

The element <ResponsabilitiesAudit> delegates the responsible individuals, that will legally answer during the auditing, as well as the auditor responsible for the <ReportRecommendation>.

1.1.6) DocumentAnalises

The element <DocumentAnalises> is responsible for containing instances of the documents to be critically analyzed. It must be taken into consideration the size, complexity and nature of the organization, as well as the <ObjectivAudit> and the <EscopeAudit>. Only verifiable data may be selected for analysis.

1.1.7) LogFindings

<LogFindings> stores the log of the findings of the process, being able to point out the conformity or unconformity of <DocumentAnalises> in respect to <CriterionAudit>.

1.1.8) ReportRecommendation

The element <ReportRecommendation> is sent after the analysis of the element <LogFindings> and based on the unconformities that were evidenced a report containing a description of them, as well as the element <CriterionAudit> regarding the unconformities found and their degree is written.

The degrees are divided in two, namely:

- Simple Degree: Simple fault that does not compromise the integrity of the financial report, but requires improvements in order to avoid making its usage impossible;
- High Degree: Major fault that compromises the integrity of the financial report, rendering it unusable.

1.1.9) PlanAction

The element <PlanAction> is set to solve possible faults pointed out, by attributing actions and their respective responsible parts that will have to monitor their completion.

1.1.10) AuditArc

The element <AuditArc> establishes a connection arc between the <Locator> and the <AuditTechnique>.

1.1.10.1) Conformity

<Conformity> is a subelement of <AuditArc>, which expresses the conformity level established by the connection between <Locator> and <AuditTechnique>.

V. CONCLUSION, LIMITATIONS AND FUTURE WORKS

The xAudit specification proposal has, as an objective, solve the shortage of auditing standards for XBRL data, thus contributing positively for the consolidation of the XBRL standard and its utilization. Important aspects in an auditing process can be represented in xAudit: the responsibilization of the auditor, definition of context, type and method of auditing, conformity, action management, among others. Continuous auditing is one of the keys to improve and audit business processes. The use of adequate technology directly influences the achievement of better results, real-time verification and accurate data analysis, in this case, a use of xAudit will be of great value in this task. xAudit creates a layer of software for representation of auditing processes, and with that, it is expected that auditing software administration can execute its processes in a standardized fashion.

This work is currently still in the concept definition stage, the following stages will consist of the specification definition, creation of a taxonomy based in auditing regulations and xAudit, the development of an application that opens the doors for the executing of auditing based on a real case study and verifying the performance of said auditing.

xAudit is a proposal for the improvement of current auditing processes, to be of use as a tool for the auditing process in XBRL-formatted files.

REFERENCES

[1] Miklos A. Vasarhelyi e David Y. Chan, "Innovation and Practice of Continuous," em *Continuous Auditing: Theory and Application*, 2006, pp. 271-283.

[2] *Brazilian Association of Technical Standards, NBR ISO 19011 - Guidelines for audits of quality and / or environmental management system,* Rio de Janeiro: ABNT, 2012.

[3] AICPA, "*SEC Rules for Reporting Financial Statements in XBRL Format*," [accessed: 05, 2018]. Available: https://www.aicpa.org/interestareas/frc/accountingfinancialreporting/xbrl/secrulesforreportingfinancialstatementsinxbrlformat.html.

[4] OSLER, "Osler," [accessed: 05, 2018]. Available: https://www.osler.com/en/resources/regulations/2017/sec-tags-public-companies-using-ifrs-with-xbrl-r.

[5] XBRL International, "XBRL International's Point of View - Proposal to ISO for New work item proposal - Audit data collection," New Work, 2015.

[6] M. A. . P. Silva e P. C. Silva, "Analytical Processing for Forensic Analysis.," *IEEE 18th International Enterprise Distributed Object Computing Conference Workshops and Demonstrations.*, p. 364 – 371, 2014.

[7] XBRL International, "XBRL," [accessed: 05, 2018]. Available: http://xbrl.org.

[8] ISO, "*International Organization for Standardization*," [Online]. Available: https://www.iso.org/technical-committees.html. [accessed: 05, 2018].

[9] S. Mardian, *XBRL, How it implies the audit process,* 2106.

[10] J.L.Geraldo, Data Model for Sped Based on XBRL GL, Bahia, 2015.

[11] K. Hasenstab, *Extracting your company's data with the new audit data standard.*

[12] XBRL International, "XBRL Specification 2.1," 2013. Available: http://specifications.xbrl.org/work-product-index-group-base-spec-base-spec.html. [accessed: 05, 2018].

[13] National Treasury Secretariat of Brazil. Available:https://siconfi.tesouro.gov.br/siconfi/index.jsf . [accessed: 05, 2018].

[14] United Nations Auditing Regulations. Available: http://www1.unece.org/cefact/platform/display/TBG/TBG12. [accessed: 05, 2018].

[15] Swedish SIE. Available: http://www.sie.se. [accessed: 05, 2018].

[16] Dutch Auditfile Financieel. Available: http://www.softwarepakket.nl/swpakketten/auditfiles/auditfile_financieel.php?bronw=1. [accessed: 05, 2018].

[17] XBRL Generic Links. Available: http://www.xbrl.org/Specification/gnl/rec-2009-06-22/gnl-rec-2009-06-22.html. [accessed: 05, 2018].

[18] XBRL International Consortium. Available: http://xbrl.org. [accessed: 05, 2018].

[19] World Wide Web Consortium. Available: https://www.w3.org/. [accessed: 05, 2018].

[20] Group of Research in Software Engineering and Applications (GESA). http://dgp.cnpq.br/dgp/espelhogrupo/2178422134545563. [accessed: 05, 2018].

[21] XBRLFramework Group. https://xbrlframework.wordpress.com. [accessed: 05, 2018].

Value Engineering and Agile for building Urgent and Emergency Care

Daniela America da Silva, Samara Cardoso dos Santos, Wilson Cristoni, Luiz Coura, Fabio Kfouri, Gildarcio Sousa Goncalves, Alyson Basilio, Ricardo Alvarenga, Breslei Max Reis da Fonseca, Jean Carlos Lourenco Costa, Juliana F. Pasquini Martinez, Claudio Lima, Alexandre Nascimento, Johnny Marques, Luiz Alberto Vieira Dias, Adilson Marques da Cunha, Paulo Marcelo Tasinaffo
Electronic Engineering and Computing Department
Brazilian Aeronautics Institute of Technology
São José dos Campos, São Paulo, Brazil
Email: stagiho-bd@googlegroups.com

Abstract—**In health care, combating waste is an emerging issue as clinicians face the complexities of current patient care requiring to apply new technologies as also collaborate with professionals from engineering and computer science background. Answering to that call, during the 1st Semester of 2018, at the Brazilian Aeronautics Institute of Technology (Instituto Tecnológico de Aeronautica - ITA), a successful Collaborative Interdisciplinary Problem-Based Learning (Co-IPBL) experience took place, for conceptualizing, modeling, developing, and testing a Computer System based upon Big Data, Blockchain Hyperledger, Micro-services, and other emerging technologies applied to Urgent and Emergency Care. The Co-IPBL experience had the participation of a medical technical team from the Hospital of Clinics at the Faculty of Medicine of the University of São Paulo. In the present article, we discuss how value engineering, agile and the business model canvas could help improve functionality benefit, reduce cost, combat waste and reduce complexity. We then propose a process to apply a quantitative method to prioritize valuable User Stories, reducing scope and demonstrating real delivered value as proposed in the Business Model Canvas. For the implementation, the Blockchain Hyperledger was used as a common database of health care information that doctors and providers could access.**

Keywords-Health Care System; Big Data; Internet of Things; Agile method and testing; Intelligent Systems; Micro-services Architecture; Cloud Computing; Blockchain; interdisciplinarity; Collaborative problem-based learning.

I. INTRODUCTION

This paper tackles the development of an academic project using the Collaborative Interdisciplinary Problem-Based Learning (Co-IPBL) and how value engineering, agile and the business model canvas could help to improve functionality benefit, increase the effectiveness of attendance in hospital and/or reducing cost for the specific urgent and emergency care domain.

Combating waste is a permanent goal and priority of all organizations. Any activity in the project that is not adding some value or utility to someone is an unnecessary activity and must be eliminated. Another area requiring attention is the capacity and human energy, and the waste of these capabilities has brought huge losses to companies. Combating waste is a responsibility everyone can not be left out of it, because non-participation is already a waste of a very valuable resource, which is human talent.

In health care, combating waste is an emerging issue as clinicians face the complexities of current patient care: the need for applying new technologies in health care management and the need for health care professionals to collaborate with professionals from engineering and computer science background. Interdisciplinary health care teams with members from many professions and value engineering usually answer calls, by working together, collaborating, communicating closely and improving functionality benefits to digitize patients' care [10]-[12].

This research work provides an integration of 3 different courses taught at the Brazilian Aeronautics Institute of Technology (*Instituto Tecnológico de Aeronáutica - ITA*): CE-240 Database Systems Projects, CE-245 Information Technologies, and CE-229 Software Testing. It involved some cooperative work with technical Physicians from Urgent and Emergency Health Care at the Hospital of Clinics from the Faculty of Medicine at the University of São Paulo, Brazil.

This academic project was driven by ITA to generate expertise on developing, integrating, and managing Urgent and Emergency Health Care in the Hospital of Clinics [4]. This project was named in Portuguese *Soluções Tecnológicas Aplicáveis ao Gerenciamento de Informações Hospitalares Ostensivas com Big Data - STAGIHO-DB*, meaning in English, "Technological Solutions Applicable for Managing Ostensive Hospital Information with Big Data-TSA4MOHIBD". Scrum Agile Method [1]-[3], Value Engineering [15][16], Business Model Canvas[19] and its best practices were used, in order to develop a computer system to satisfy project requirements in a time frame of just 16 academic weeks.

This TSA4MOHIBD Project [5] was divided into two groups of application: External Regulation and Internal Regulation, by sharing its development among four student teams, which were responsible for developing different functional requirements involving the verification of quality, reliability, safety, and testability.

This research work project was developed by using GitHub to store program code, NodeJs [21] for the development of Java Micro-services (fine-grained services), NoSQL Databases [22] to store the internal data for the Hospital, Blockchain Hyperledger [9] to store the electronic health records, Kafka [23] for message exchanging in the common communication data bus, and other emerging technologies. During this collaborative project development, more than 20 students have practiced the roles of Product Owner (PO), Scrum Masters (SMs), and Team Developers (TDs).

At the end of this project, a total of 52 Atributtes has been identified to prepare 35 User Stories (USs) to compose the Product Backlog. However, only 20 USs were developed within 3 monthly sprints as part of scope reduction and value engineering. For each Sprint was built a Business Model Canvas describing the benefits to be delivered. In the first week of each sprint it was performed the Sprint Planning to identify the USs aligned with the Business Model Canvas, and every week the development process was monitored to keep the focus on the big picture and final product more aligned to target audience desires and needs [19]. At the end of each sprint, reviews and retrospective meetings took place. Moreover, the Acceptance Test Driven Development (ATDD) [6] was applied by generating a minimum, necessary, and sufficient set of artifacts stored at the Project Internet Portal [5].

For each US, more than one test case and acceptance test were developed. The integration strategy between groups of subsystem components occurred, by using Micro-services, a Commom Data Communication Bus, and Blockchain Hyperledger, allowing information to be available via broadcast to every hospital area and also to the External Regulator named CROSS (named in Portuguese *Central de Regulação de Ofertas de Serviços de Saúde* and meaning in English the Regulation Center for Health Services Offerings).

An overview of the Urgent and Emergency Care flow is presented in Figure 1.

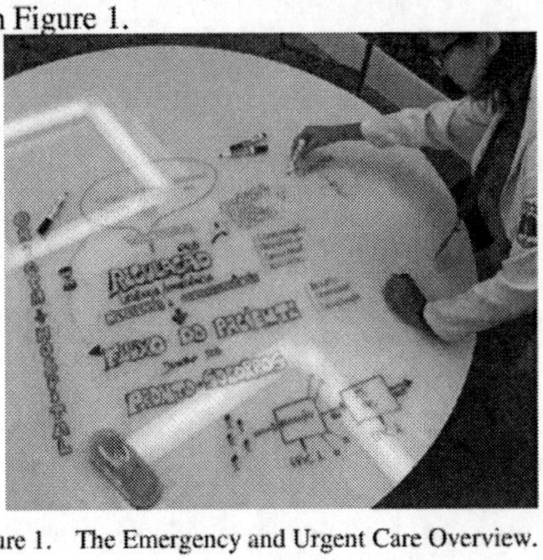

Figure 1. The Emergency and Urgent Care Overview.

In Section II, we describe the attributes of Urgent and Emergency Care at the HCFMUSP. In Section III we present the analysis of attributes and the process applied to reduce scope prioritizing the most valuable USs according to the Value Engineering analysis. In Section IV, we present the Proof of Concept. In Section V, we present the final deliverables using Blockchain Hyperledger. And in Section VI we state our conclusions and suggest possible topics for future research.

II. The Urgency and Emergency Health Care In the HCFMUSP

Before starting the academic year, some students from the Brazilian Aeronautics Institute of Technology (ITA) had a planning meeting with some members of the Emergency Care in the Hospital of Clinics from the Faculty of Medicine at the University of São Paulo (in Portuguese, *Hospital da Clínicas da Faculdade de Medicina de São Paulo - HCFMUSP)*.

On that opportunity, the internal members of the hospital have presented some details of the internal and external regulation and clarified the diagram presented in Figure 1. At that time, there was also an on-site visit to some emergency areas and hospital sectors and it was agreed that some information should be shared with ITA developers, such as students and professors, in order to provide requirements specifications for the next steps of project development.

A. Regulations

Regulations of Hospitals and Health Units attending Urgencies and Emergencies are usually carried out by the Health Care Supply Regulatory Center (CROSS). Some urgencies and emergencies are referred to the CROSS by: the Mobile Emergency Response Service (in Portuguese, *Serviço de Atendimento Móvel de Urgência - SAMU*); the Military Police Operations Center (in Portuguese, *Central de Operações Policias Militares - COPOM*); the Firefighter Operations Center (in Portuguese, *Centro de Operações do Corpo de Bombeiros - COBOM*); and/or Health, Secondary Hospitals, and Specialized Hospitals.

It is through the CROSS that the HCFMUSP use to be contacted, in order to respond to urgencies and emergencies. An emergency patient may also arrive by the regular entrance of the HCFMUSP and after contacting the CROSS (usually via email or through the CROSS Web Portal), the HCFMUSP will screen through an Internal Hospital Regulation to filter relevant cases for hospital care.

B. The External Regulation

The Health Care Secretary of São Paulo understood the regulation as an important tool for the management of public health systems, which has among its objectives the equity of the access implemented through dynamic actions executed in an equitable, orderly, timely and rational way, creating the CROSS, which brings together actions aimed at regulating access in hospitals and outpatient areas, contributing to the integrality of the assistance, providing the adjustment of the available health care supply to the immediate needs of the citizen as described at the CROSS Internet Portal [13].

C. The Internal Regulation

The Internal Regulation is the area responsible in the Hospital for verifying availability to receive a Patient and will also make the contact with the appropriate hospital institute to evaluate if a Patient could be transferred to the Hospital.

III. THE BUSINESS MODEL CANVAS

The Business Model Canvas is a simple graphical template describing nine essential components and it brings clarity and simplicity to evaluate business models in minutes [19] and a way to refocus the way you view your business. Between the elements analyzed are: Customer segments, value propositions, channels, customer relationships (such as self-service or personal assistance), revenue streams, resources, activities, partnerships, and costs.

The individual elements prompt consideration of a business' full scope, while the layout encourages thought about how the pieces fit together. In Figure 2 is presented the Urgent and Emergency Care Business Model Canvas. And in Table I and II the details analyzed for each Business Canvas Element.

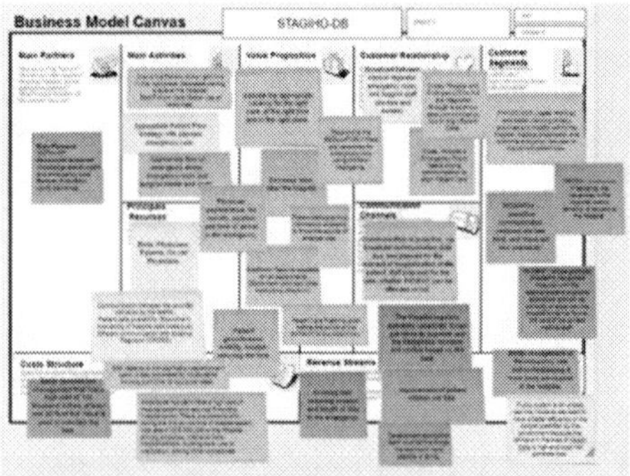

Figure 2. The Urgent and Emergency Care Business Model Canvas

TABLE I. THE BUSINESS MODEL CANVAS - MAPPING RESOURCES

Elements	Urgent and Emergency Care
Main Partners	HCFMUSP. Resources acquired: Knowledge about urgent and emergency care. Partner Activities: Verify deliveries.
Main Activities	Attend the Patient at the right time in the right place. Decrease waiting queue at the Hospital. Best Patient Care. Better use of resources. Appropriate Patient Flow Strategy with planned emergency care. Appropriate flow of emergency doors, emergency room and surgical center and costs.
Main resources	Beds, Physicians, Patients, On Call Physicians. Communication between the services delivered by the teams. Patient data availability (Blockchain). Availability of hospital data (data bus). Efficient communication with External Regulator (CROSS)

TABLE II. THE BUSINESS MODEL CANVAS - MAPPING VALUES

Elements	Urgent and Emergency Care
Value proposition	Allocate the appropriate vacancy for the right care, at the right time and in the right place. Respond to the REGULATOR if there are vacancies for emergency care using Artificial Intelligence. Decrease silos within the hospital. Patient demographics information available to know the source of emergencies. Physician georeference, his mobility, location and time of arrival in the emergency. Patient georeference, mobility, location, reducing idle time. Health Care Planning even before the arrival of the PATIENT to the HOSPITAL. Electronic Records available for all departments (Blockchain) and also other institutions (check-in).
Customer Relationship	Broadcast between internal regulator, emergency room, and support staff (doctors and nurses). Cross, Hospital and Emergency First Aid are integrated through a common data communication bus to align Patient Care. Patient data is in BlockChain.
Communication Channels	Communication is proactive, via broadcast communication data bus, bed planned for the moment of hospitalization of the patient, staff prepared for the care. The communication is proactive, the Hospital regularly publishes vacancies, Cross publishes its requests and the intelligence monitors and verifies based on this data whether PATIENT can be attended or not.
Customer Segments	CROSS - It will know in advance the vacancies in the Hospital, before sending a request to the Hospital. PHYSICIANS - better informed and better planning of daily activities and mobility within the hospital, medical prescription and outcome evaluation, focused on the correct patient care. HOSPITAL - proactive communication, reduced idle bed time, and improved bed availability. PATIENT - will be promptly directed to the correct Hospital, with the appropriate and available specialists and will be promptly directed into the hospital's internal flow to the care of the correct medical staff.
Costs Structure	Better hospital bed management that has a high cost of 150 thousand dollars at least and 40% of this value is used to maintain the bed. Motorcycle Accident have a high cost of hospitalization and requires 6 months hospitalization. There are patients who, during the first six months of hospitalization, cost about R\$ 600,000 to the Hospital, among surgeries, Intensive Care hospitalizations, nursing care, use of medication, among other procedures. With regards to the application development team, it was composed by 23 students working part time 10 hours per week.
Revenue Streams	Avoiding loss, reducing evasion and length of stay in the emergency. Improvement of patient rotation per bed. Better management of the occupancy rate and understanding if more beds are needed in the Hospital. Public system is an unpaid service, however we need to have a better efficiency of the budget predicted by the government because the demand in the area of Health Care is high and must not generate loss. Development application team must do the things the team said were capable of doing.

IV. VALUE ENGINEERING

A. *Analyzing Urgency and Emergency Care Attributes*

In order to collect data, a visit to the HCFMUSP was carried out, and documents provided by the Hospital were collected to provide initial understanding on the flow of care from the CROSS service request until the patient arrived at the Hospital and patient care started. The adoption of the meeting with the technical team is justified to identify the team's perception of the current service operation and the opportunities for improvement.

The people of the HCFMUSP technical team selected for the meeting are those who participate in the internal regulation of the hospital for patient care authorization: the director of internal regulation, and two physicians who coordinate the internal regulation. The people from the ITA selected for the meeting were one PhD Candidate student and one Master's degree student for the preparation of the requirements specification.

As a result, it was possible to understand the characteristics of urgent and emergency service assigning degrees of importance to each service attribute. On top of most valuable attributes, to simplify the Proof of Concept and to reduce the scope and complexity of the system to be developed, a mission assigned was developed to the rescue of motorcycle accident victims, mainly because it is a frequent occurrence in the city of São Paulo [17][18].

The Definition of Ready (DoR) checklist was created to indicate to the team that the US was READY to be INITIATED, that is, all necessary definitions, information, data and resources have been provided, UNDERSTOOD and ESTIMATED, and the development and testing phase can be initiated.

The Definition of Done (DoD) checklist was created and tells the team that the US is READY to be DELIVERED, that is, all development and testing activities have been performed. Without the DoD the US can not be considered delivered to the Product Owner.

The User Stories were written using the INVEST (Independent, Negotiable, Valuable, Estimable, Small, Testable) method because it solves practically the entire DoR. If US does not meet DoR's requirements, it can not be placed on the Sprint Backlog. Also, team members did not wait for Sprint Planning to prepare the next US, it was done constantly and the Product Backlog was updated according to the expected benefit to be delivered during the Sprint. The USs that comply with the DoR were placed at the top of the Product Backlog, according to the example in Figure 3 below.

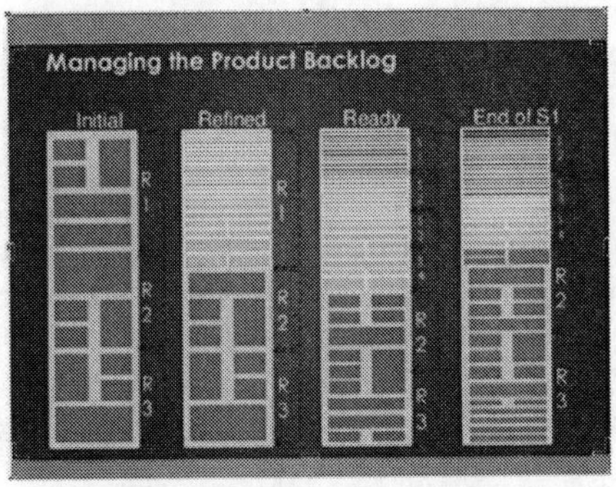

Figure 3. Managing the Product Backlog

Table III and IV presents details of scope reduction, from the identification of attributes to the deliverable of a product propitiating good benefits to the Urgent and Emergency Care, and specifically for the External Regulation, from the request placed by CROSS for Patient Care, to Hospital vacancy and confirmation of acceptance from the Hospital.

TABLE III. THE EXTERNAL REGULATION SCOPE REDUCTION - MAIN STEPS

Attributes	Quantity	Valuable for USs	Scope reduction	USs Developed
About Patient Care	10	5	3	1
About Logistics	6	1	1	1
About the Internal Controller	10	6	5	3
About the Governance	8	7	2	2
About the Standards	5	0	0	0
About Systems Integration	14	5	4	2
About the Management of Beds	4	2	2	2
TOTAL	60	26	17	9

TABLE IV. THE EXTERNAL REGULATION SCOPE REDUCTION - INTERACTIONS

Attributes	Quantity	Valuable for USs	Scope reduction	USs Developed
About Data Quality	4	3	2	1
About the Human Factor	1	0	0	0
About the Telemedicine	2	2	2	0
About the Hierarchy	2	1	0	0
TOTAL	9	6	4	1

Table V presents details of scope reduction specifically for the Internal Regulation from the response to the CROSS confirming Patient Acceptance to the Patient identification, arrival and care after arrival in the Hospital propitiating good benefits to the Hospital Internal Health Care Flow.

TABLE V. THE INTERNAL REGULATION SCOPE REDUCTION

Attributes	Quantity	Valuable for USs	Scope reduction	USs Developed
About the Lobby	5	2	1	1
About the Identification	8	5	3	3
About Patient Care	7	3	1	1
About Patients in the Emergency Room	5	2	1	1
About the Internal Flow of Patients	3	2	1	1
About the Internal Flow of Physicians	4	1	1	1
About the Internal Flow of Nurses	2	1	1	0

Attributes	Quantity	Valuable for USs	Scope reduction	USs Developed
Integration Needs	11	4	4	2
TOTAL	45	20	14	10

In Figure 4, it is presented a chart demonstrating how the value engineering, agile method and business model canvas combined could simplify the Proof of Concept and reduce the scope and complexity of the system to be developed, and demonstrates that developing team managed to choose USs that could delivery the benefits mapped in the Business Model Canvas presented in Table I and II and how this process based on value could reduce complexity in developing phase.

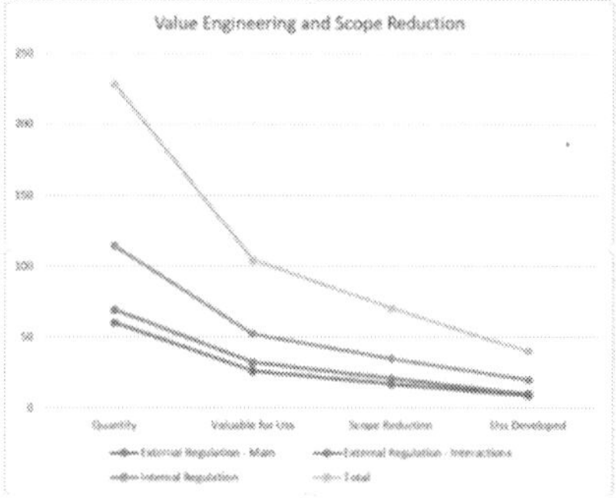

Figure 4. The Value Engineering Results and the Scope Reduction

Figure 5 presents a summary on the Urgent and Emergency Care deliverables based on the Value Engineering Analysis. It demonstrates that value could be increased focusing in improving process to propitiate the right Patient to the correct Patient Care, proactive communication with Regulator, sharing vacancies prior to receive requests, improving speed to plan and predict Patient Care and sharing Patient Information to internal institutes and other Institutions through blockchain [20].

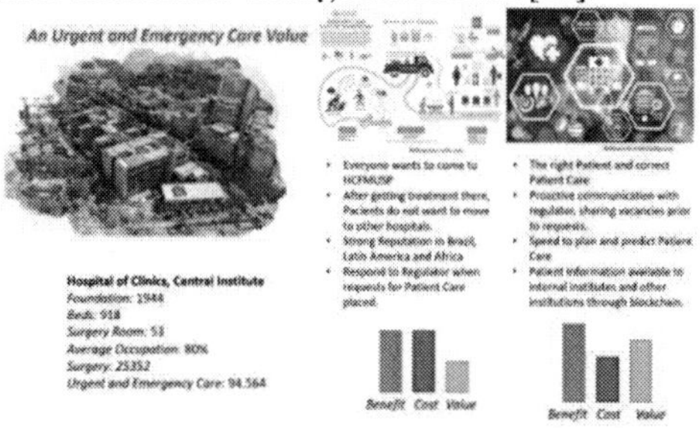

Figure 5. An Urgent and Emergency Health Care Value

As presented in Figure 6, for the external regulation the team focused on USs related to communication between CROSS and Internal Controller, Governance, Systems Integration, Management of Hospital Beds, and Data Quality using Blockchain.

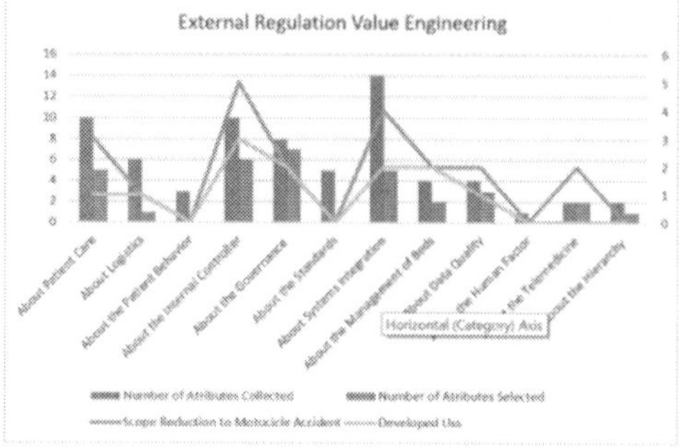

Figure 6. External Regulation Value Engineering

And as presented in Figure 7 for the internal regulation the team focused on USs related to patient identification, planning and managing patient care in the emergency room, managing flow of Patient and Physicians in the Hospital, and improving integration needs using blockchain.

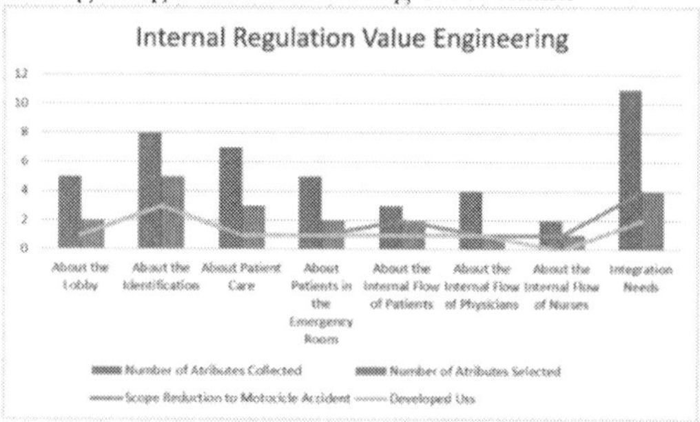

Figure 7. Internal Regulation Value Engineering

B. The Proof of Concept as an Assigned Mission

To reduce the scope and complexity of the system to be developed, a mission assigned was developed to the rescue of motorcycle accident victims, mainly because it is a frequent occurrence in the city of São Paulo. On a regular workday, every 15 minutes, the SAMU assists a motorcyclist in the city of São Paulo. Most of victims are not made up of motoboys. Usually, they are drivers who use vehicles (motorbikes) to go to work or are weekend drivers. Rehabilitation of those who are injured is usually time-consuming and laborious, as described below:

- 40\% of motorcycle accident victims need to undergo complex surgeries and long physiotherapy treatments;
- The most serious injuries caused by motorcycle accidents are usually in the skull and spine;
- Most motorcycle riders use the vehicle as transport, only for 2 hours a day, usually to move between home and work place; Most of them have been injured before;
- Of the total number of accidents initially investigated, 2% resulted in death of motorcyclists;
- Of the total number of injuries: 48% had serious injuries, 17% in the legs and feet; 12% in arms; and 23% had other types of trauma;
- Most of them were discharged immediately after care and only 18% had to be hospitalized; and

- Considering the annual costs, about R$ 100 million are invested by the Orthopedics Institute of the HC, exclusively for the recovery of motorcyclists: "These are patients who, in the first six months of hospitalization, cost about R$ 300 thousands to the Hospital, on surgeries, ICU hospitalizations, occupations of wards, use of medications, among other procedures.

Based on previously reported motorcycle accident data, the development of the TSA4MOHIBD project should be able to provide an adequate management for the control of victim assistance only considering motorcycle accidents, in such a way that:

- Those motorcycle accident victims (PATIENTS) may be appropriately diagnosed, promptly identified and/or attended to;

- PHYSICIANS may have computers and/or computer tools capable of providing preventive and appropriate planning, scheduling, and controlling of motorcycle accident emergency services, for example, identifying the needs of: hospitalization time; procedures; medical teams; procedures for surgery preparations; as well as the availability of operating rooms and Intensive Therapy Units;

- The HOSPITAL and/or the INTERNAL CONTROLLER shall have computers and/or computer tools capable of using appropriate technologies to provide efficient screening methods, prioritization of care, patient and physician locations within the HOSPITAL, in order to locate, if necessary, other HOSPITALS to attend emergencies of motorcycle accident victims, according to the criticalities and needs from specialized treatments of the PATIENTS;

- HOSPITAL must have adequate computers and/or computer means to collaborate in the process of managing large data flows, involving efficient attendance of injured motorcycle patients, by using appropriate technologies and efficient screening methods for this type of emergency;

- SUPPLIERS of medicines, devices and/or technologies must have appropriate tools to participate in logistics and/or supply process to be used in care and/or care for victims from motorcycle accidents attended by urgent and emergency care of HOSPITALS;

- PHYSICIANS and NURSES must have appropriate tools to provide care to victims from motorcycle accidents attended by the urgent and emergency care of the HOSPITAL, for example, to identify them from their entrance hall, by verifying and controlling also the movement of the stretchers, according to internal flows of required services;

- Each confirmed case of motorcycle-injured PATIENT can and should generate, within the inventory control of a HOSPITAL, the release of care kits containing materials and medications, according to the size of events. In these cases, in addition to medicines, other supplies can and should be considered important, such as blood bags for transfusions, as accident victims need quick rescue and motorcycle accidents kill from blood loss;

- The population/society should have access to computers and/or computer tools of the System Project involving the TSA4MOHIBD and/or the Real-time TSA4MOHIBD capable of providing appropriate records, management, controls, and governance of resources used in the area of Health Care;

- Public administration must have reliable data to provide a comprehensive situational awareness to support decision making for accidents and/or crises, involving motorcycle accidents.

V. The Final Product

In order to provide appropriate speed in the communication with the Regulator and also to allow the Regulator to know in advance the number of bed vacancy in the Hospital, it is suggested that the communication between the Regulator and the Hospital works similarly to the AirBnB model. Then, the hospital will publish in a data bus communication how many vacancy, physicians, and specialists are available and also the Regulator will publish an attendance request for a patient and its initial conditions.

After that, an Artificial Intelligence algorithm will perform some analysis to identify what kind of treatment is necessary for the Patient, and to search among the Hospitals which one is closest, has a vacancy and suitable resources to receive this Patient. The Artificial Intelligence algorithm, after finding the appropriate Hospital, will place in the same data bus a message to the Hospital.

In the Hospital at the Internal Regulator, the operator will analyze the request and through the application system the operator will place a message in the Data Bus, by informing to Artificial Intelligence algorithm that the Patient was accepted and will inform straight the Urgent Care Unit that a Patient will arrive, also informing the date and time of the estimated arrival. The patient information will be available in the Blockchain Hyperledger, and then data from the CROSS and also data about the Patient will be internally matched in the Hospital. From that point onwards, the planning for Patient Care will be started prior to the Patient arrival.

When the Patient arrives the technical team, the bed, and the required examination and health care steps will proceed as per suggested planning. After acceptance from the Internal Controller, the intelligence of the system will place a message to the Regulator, by informing that the Patient was accepted by the HCFMUSP.

After a Patient arrived at the Hospital, his Electronic Health Record could be read by any Institute or professional from inside of the HCFMUSP, and information about patient care steps, as all the current bed management in the Hospital, would be presented through a dashboard that could be available for the governance team, by physicians and nurses looking at the next steps of the Patient Care.

For the Urgency and Emergency Care at the HCFMUSP, our proposal is to use two separate Blockchain networks: one for Patient and other for Attendance. The Blockchain Patient network has overall patient information and is a private network with information that can be accessed by the CROSS and any other Institution that would like in the future to access Patient Identification (e.g., Single Health System, in Portuguese, named *Sistema Único de Saúde - SUS*). The Blockchain Attendance network has detailed patient information and all the heath care details performed by the Hospital. And it is a private network with information that can be accessed only by the Hospital and internal institutes. For future work, examination details could be also stored in this Blockchain network.

The main benefit of isolating patient's data from patient's own care is to provide data safety, since confidential information will be managed only by the hospital. The indirect benefit is to allow that two different groups of students learning Blockchain could also learn separately and then the integration has worked smoothly during the Sprint 3 of the TSA4MOHIBD project, focusing in the Integration.

The Blockchain Hyperledger implementation also makes use of encapsulated micro-services allowing smooth functionalities' integrations, which were developed during Sprint 1, focusing in the External Flow implementation, and Sprint 2, focusing in the Internal Flow Implementation. The overview of The Proposed Product Architecture is presented in Figure 8.

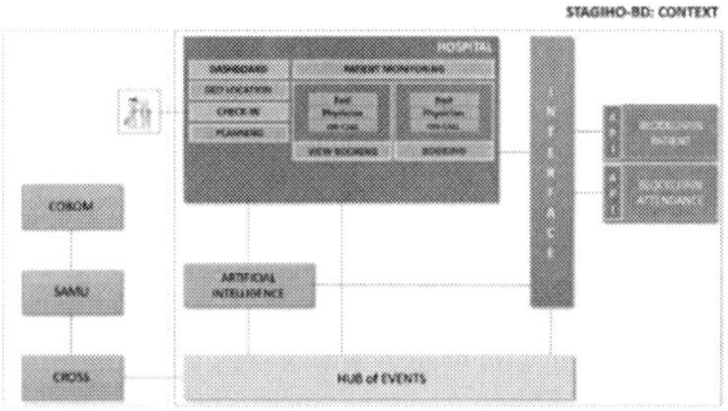

Figure 8. The Proposed Architecture Overview

VI. Conclusion

This paper aimed to describe the development of an academic interdisciplinary project combining Scrum agile method, value engineering and the business model canvas in order to develop a prototype for a Proof of Concept (PoC) to improve functionality benefit and/or reducing cost in the urgent and emergency care domain.

It has described a Collaborative Integrated Problem-Based Learning (Co-IPBL) performed with the participation of a medical technical team from the Hospital of Clinics from the Faculty of Medicine of the University of São Paulo (in Portuguese, *Hospital das Clínicas da Faculdade de Medicina de São Paulo - HCFMUSP*), focusing in the Urgent and Emergency Care. This academic research project was named in Portuguese as "*Soluções Tecnológicas Aplicáveis ao Gerenciamento de Informações Hospitalares Ostensivas com Big Data - STAGIHO-DB*", meaning in English, "Technological Solutions Applicable for the Management of Ostensive Hospital Information with Big Data - TSA4MOHIBD", a Computer System based on Big Data, Blockchain Hyperledger, Micro-services, and other emerging technologies for governmental organization and private sector.

The purpose of this system was to aggregate data and integrate sectors, such as External and Internal Regulations through its PATIENTS, HOSPITALS, PHYSICIANS, and HEALTH CARE SUPPLIERS, for the decision making process related to Urgency and Emergency Care, involving motorcycle accidents. The TSA4MOHIBD project was developed by students from three different Computer Science courses taught at the Brazilian Aeronautics Institute of Technology (*Instituto Tecnológico de Aeronáutica – ITA*), on the 1st Semester of 2018.

A. *Specific Conclusions*

The use of interdisciplinary in 3 courses of Computer Science has worked as expected, since students were able to know how to work in teams to successfully develop a complex computer system.

The cloud-computing environment has been widely used by students to enable collaborative work from distance, by using remote meetings, personal websites, and an official project website. The Scrum framework has been adapted to the reality of the interdisciplinary academic environment of ITA, helping the entire team of more than 20 students to offer value to stakeholders at the end of each sprint and also at the end of this project.

Combating waste is a permanent goal and priority of this project as well active participation of team members, since human talent is a very valuable resource. The Collaborative Interdisciplinary and the use of Value Engineering and Business Canvas propitiate identify the valuable functionality to be developed during the Proof of Concept and the benefits desired for the Urgent and Emergency Care. And the process increased creativity in the use of disruptive technologies and in the use of innovative practices in software development.

The application of Test Driven Development (TDD) and Acceptance Testing Driven Development (ATDD) techniques in the project was closely related to the interdisciplinary approach adopted, since acceptance tests were created by CE-229 Software Testing course students, while the Blockchain, NodeJS applications, and the Value Engineering and Business Model Canvas were implemented by CE-240 Database System Project and CE-245 Information Technologies course students.

Its operating logic was established and all teams were able to perform development integration, by defining and accomplishing the phases of an Assigned Mission to reduce scope, mapping User Stories to functionalities for the External and Internal regulations integration, which variables and detailed characteristics would be changed as inputs and/or outputs. The main results obtained from the use of the TSA4MOHIBD project prototype were successful.

At the end of this project, in just 17 weeks, it was possible to demonstrate the building of the Collaborative Interdisciplinary Project TSA4MOHIBD, without completeness, but following a model with quality, reliability, safety, testability, norms, and standards applicable to a product of this nature. Finally, students have presented the TSA4MOHIBD Academic Project Prototype, as the final project for their courses, as a Proof of Concept (PoC) to professors, entrepreneurs, and some invited guests from industry and academia.

B. General Conclusions

The academic development of a critical intelligent system is a rewarding experience that can be used in different undergrad and graduate courses. The use of interdisciplinary, Blockchain Hyperledger, cloud computing, value engineering, business model canvas, and agile methods seems to be an interesting novel and exciting way to achieve academic goals, in just one semester of 17 weeks and can also be extended to other knowledge domains.

It is possible to avoid waste and increase value by either improving the functionality benefits and/or reduce costs. The technique applied uses rational logic and analysis of functionalities, modern technologies and agile practices to increase value. The Proof of Concept demonstrates the importance of customer perception of value, the business goals, needs and issues to build the best solution. It also propitiated keep the focus on the big picture prioritizing first the most important functionalities, better support for business decisions, points out waste that could be eliminated, speed up solution delivery, and promoted better communication, alignment and commitment between project team members.

C. Recommendations

It is strongly recommended to align expectations and results that may be compromised and quickly adjusted to review deliverables, when working with emerging technologies. This cycle, in the area of computing science, should be repeated all the time we have to deal with new technologies. It is important to have on the team participants who will face the challenge of learning and preparing a legacy.

It is also fundamental to have participants in the team that could identify in advance were the team could fail with the new technology, proposing improvements and allowing the team to repositioning itself to deliver what is agreed in consensus in the appropriate time.

The business model canvas produced presented a summary on the valuable functionality for the Urgent and Emergency Care, and for an investor view it is recommended to prepare a simplified Business Model Canvas that focus on cost reduction. While using new technologies, such as Blockchain and Node JS, it is important to build tutorials to speed up team members learning curve.

It is recommended the continuation of this Project, by starting from what has already been done, possible to obtain and execute, within the courses on the next semesters, on new Sprints, generating the possibility of increasing completeness.

D. Future Work

It is suggested that the process used in this TSA4MOHIBD academic project prototype can be extended to other Agile projects, in order to improve estimation of efforts, resources and avoid waste to attend Urgent and Emergency Care. It is also suggested the use of some simulation processes to measure Urgent and Emergency Care with and without the use of Value Engineering supporting projects development in health care.

Finally, for future work, it is suggested to expand some cooperation among the ITA, hospitals, innovation foundations, medical suppliers, industries and public and private enterprises, in order to get a selection of academic projects aligned to updated needs from the market.

ACKNOWLEDGMENT

The authors would like to thank the Hospital of Clinics from The Faculty of Medicine at The University of São Paulo, the Brazilian Aeronautics Institute of Technology, the Ecossistema Negócios Digitais Ltda for its finantial support and scholarships, during the STAMPS Project Development and The Casimiro Montenegro Filho Foundation (FCMF) for their support, during the development of this TSA4MOHIBD Project.

REFERENCES

[1] J. Sutherland, "SCRUM Handbook", Scrum Training Institute Press, 2010

[2] D. Cohen et al., "An Introduction to Agile Methods", Fraunhofer Center for Experimental Software Engineering, ADVANCES IN COMPUTERS, VOL. 62, 2004.

[3] M. Cohn, "Succeeding with agile: Software development using Scrum", 1st Edition, Pearson Education, Inc., 2010.

[4] FMUSP, "Medical School of São Paulo", 2018, accessed from http://www.fm.usp.br/fmusp/portal/ in June 10, 2018.

[5] TSA4MOHIBD Project, "Technological Solutions Applicable for the Management of Ostensive Hospital Information with Big Data", 2018, accessed from https://sites.google.com/site/projetointerdisciplinar2018/ in June 10, 2018.

[6] K. Pugh, "Lean-Agile Acceptance Test-Driven Development: Better Software Through Collaboration", Addison-Wesley, 2011, ISBN 978-0321714084.

[7] Forbes, "This is Why Blockchain will Transform HealthCare", 2017,accessed from https://www.forbes.com/sites/bernardmarr/2017/11/29/this-is-why-blockchains-will-transform-healthcare/13be90781ebe in June 10, 2018.

[8] GitHub, "Open-source landscape map for healthcare-related blockchain", 2018, accessed from https://github.com/acoravos/healthcare-blockchains in June 10, 2018.

[9] Linux Foundation Projects, "Blockchain Hyperledger", 2018, accessed from https://www.hyperledger.org/ in June 10.2018.

[10] D. A. Silva et al., "Health Care Information Systems: a Crisis Approach", In 15th International Conference on Information Technology: New Generations (ITNG 2018), 2018, Las Vegas.

[11] D. A. Silva et al., "Health Care Transformation: An Academic Application System Case Study", In 10TH IFAC Symposium on Biological and Medical Systems - International Federation of Automatic Control (IFAC BMS 2018), 2018, São Paulo, Brazil.

[12] J. C. Martins et al., "Internet of Things, and Agile for Crises Management", In 14th International Conference on Information Technology: New Generations (ITNG 2017), 2017

[13] CROSS, "Health Care Supply Regulatory Center", 2018, accessed from http://www.cross.saude.sp.gov.br/ in June 10, 2018.

[14] A. Conceicao et al., "Eletronic Health Records Using Blockchain", XXXVI Brazilian Symposium on Computer Networks and Distributed Systems (SBRC 2018), 2018, accessed from http://www.sbrc2018.ufscar.br/wp-content/uploads/2018/04/07-181717-1.pdf in June 10, 2018.

[15] P. Vieira, "Engineering and Value Analysis: a question of efficiency and survival", 2018, e-Disciplinas University of São Paulo, accessed from

https://edisciplinas.usp.br/mod/resource/view.php?id=891829 in June 10, 2018.

[16] CiT, "Presentation CiT Value Engineering Framework", 2018, accessed from https://www.ciandt.com/card/business-value-engineering-framework in June 10, 2018.

[17] M. A. B. Lima, "Target Costing in Public Hospital Services", Accounting Journal, 2013, accessed from https://periodicos.ufpe.br/revistas/ricontabeis/article/download/7966/8040 in June 10, 2018.

[18] C. Bonacim, A. Araujo, "Cost Management Applied to Public University Hospitals", Public Administration Journal, 2010, accessed from www.scielo.br/pdf/rap/v44n4/v44n4a07.pdf in June 10, 2018.

[19] Forbes, "Business Model Canvas: A Simple Tool For Designing Innovative Business Models", 2012, accessed from https://www.forbes.com/sites/tedgreenwald/2012/01/31/business-model-canvas-a-simple-tool-for-designing-innovative-business-models/ in June 10, 2018.

[20] WHO, "Emergency Care System Framework Infographic", 2018, accessed from http://www.who.int/emergencycare/emergencycare_infographic/en/ In June 10, 2018.

[21] Linux Foundation Projects, "Node.JS Foundation", 2018, accessed from https://nodejs.org/en/ in 10 June, 2018.

[22] Apache Kafka, "Apache Kafka Distributed Stream Platform", 2018,accessed from http://kafka.apache.org/

[23] MongoDB, "MongoDB", 2018, accessed from https://www.mongodb.com/